What to Do IF...

Youth Edition

The Art of Being Safe Anywhere

For Teens and Young Adult

By Douglas S. James III

DISCLAIMER

The techniques and tactics outlined in this book are intended for informational purposes only. Use them as a starting point for building ideas, plans, methods, and strategies for dealing with similar situations. The application of some of these techniques can cause severe or even fatal injury. The author and publisher of this book offer this as an informational resource and are not responsible in any manner whatsoever for any damage which may occur to anyone reading, following or trying to apply the techniques or tactics outlined herein.

Dedication

I would like to give my greatest thanks to my best friend, business partner, and beautiful wife, Barbara, who has always been beside me in all of my many adventures. I love you and look forward to many more years and adventures with you by my side. I would also like to thank my boys, Jay and Adam, for the years of training and growing together. I thank you for sharing your stories and experiences of life events that occur on college campuses. While much has changed over the years, there is still the fundamental sameness which so dictates the need for this knowledge to be shared with young adults.

-- Douglas S. James III

Acknowledgments

There are far too many people in my life that have contributed to where I am now for me to name them individually. To all of them, I give my greatest thanks. We often do not know where our sparks of inspiration come from, but for this book, I do. I would like to give great thanks to Alyssa Lorenzen whose desire to learn was the catalyst behind me writing down the information shared in this book. I must also give great thanks to my wife who realized that an email with a 35+ page attachment was a book! At times I can be a bit slow. After some discussion, I realized it was a book as well. I must also like to thank many of the teens and college students at Suwanee Choi Kwang Do. Your eagerness to learn the application of personal safety techniques demonstrated the need for this book. I want to thank my church family at Suwanee Worship Center for their support and encouragement in getting this book done. Finally, I would like to thank the many members of law enforcement that have shared their knowledge and experiences with me over the years. I hope this book reflects much of what I have learned from you.

About the Author

As an individual, I am first and foremost a Christian, then a husband, father, software designer, martial arts Instructor, and photographer. These attributes are much of what I love. The idea of being an author did not come about until the notes I was making to help with Alyssa's class got to be much more than an excessively long memo.

For many years, I have worked with and designed software for police, fire, EMS, and the military. I come by much of the knowledge in this book by riding with, talking to, and observing law enforcement officers while working to make their jobs easier. I have accompanied many officers on ride-alongs observing how they work and interact with the public and technology. As a systems designer, I dissect processes to see what I can and cannot simplify or eliminate. I approach most tasks in my life this way. This book came about when I combined the analytical processes used in software design with my love of and training in martial arts. I have been able to talk with officers across the country to learn and examine how predators work, act, and think. This book combines some practical knowledge used by officers in the field and the general public to stop would-be predators. This book also contains lessons learned from tactics that have failed, and a hefty dose of additional research to produce what I hope is a practical starting point for one's own protection.

While all authors want their work to be read and loved, I honestly hope one will never need anything in this book. Be blessed and enjoy!

Table of Contents

Introduction

About This Book

As a lifelong fan and practitioner of martial arts, I genuinely love everything about it. Whether traditional styles like Kung-Fu, Karate or modern MMA I love them all. However, the more I learned and the higher ranks I achieved, the more I realized that every self-defense class I have taken has failed to teach the fundamentals of self-defense. Yes, I can punch, strike and kick with great force. I have learned to throw a man across a room, break bones, and cause potentially fatal injuries. However, what that has taught me is what to do when every other defensive technique has failed. While I am no pacifist, I know the likely outcome of an all-out fight and would prefer to avoid such. However, there are four additional steps in the self-defense pyramid before the first push or punch. Where does one go to learn those? Who teaches how to deter a conflict before it starts? In this day and age, people of all ages need to know how not to be victims and to de-escalate a situation before violence erupts.

The core philosophy that drives my site, the **TotalWeapon.com** is to teach all the levels of the self-defense pyramid. Through demonstrations, articles, and seminars, I plan to offer a single place where teens and young adults can learn, share and grow regardless of martial arts style. This is the vision of the total-weapon project, and this is the starting point of this series of books.

Overview

While many people think of self-defense as being able to "best" another in a physical altercation, true self-defense would be better described as self-protection. It starts long before the threat of violence begins. In the best cases, one's protective techniques should prevent and deter any form of violence from ever happening. In all cases, an altercation should be the absolute last option and is a result of the failure of all other methods. This book aims to break down the tactics associated with the different levels of self- protection, to identify the causes and motivations for violence, and to build the mindset needed to prevent violence. This is not a how-to book on fighting. In fact, this is just the opposite. This book is first and foremost about avoiding being a victim of crime and violence.

Why Read This Book

I have worked to make this book easy to read. Hopefully, it will be entertaining as well. While the information contained here can apply to people of all ages, I am specifically writing this book for young people from 13 to 22. This age group is particularly vulnerable because it is a time of constant transitions and new experiences. While youth and young adults may find this time in life exciting, their desire to experience new things make them easy targets.

The subject matter, scenarios, and examples in this book include sexual assaults as well as physical violence. While there is no age limit for this material, it is my suggestion that parents and guardians read this book as well and discuss it with their children. It is my hope that this book will start discussions of self-protection by heightening one's awareness of their own vulnerabilities and inject some new ideas that will help increase one's personal safety.

Coming Soon – Family Edition

This book is targeted at young people who are experiencing new things in life and are exceptionally vulnerable to predators, but predators do not limit themselves to the young.

As I began collecting the material for this book, it became obvious that the responsibility for keeping young people safe extended far beyond the abilities of individual teens. That task includes the actions of parents, coaches, mentors, school personnel, and other caring and responsible adults charged with keeping those in their care safe. The new book will address issues such as:

- Actions adults can take to ensure their home is safe.
- Being a responsible gun owner at home and in public.
- Vetting mentors, coaches, and others that are around your family.
- How to be a good mentor and ensure that the youth in your care feel comfortable, secure, and protected?
- What acts can adults and families do to ensure safety in various situations?

Finally, **The Family Edition** addresses safety issues that are of concerns to adults, whether they have a family or not. For these reasons the second book, "**What to do If... – Family Edition.**" is already in the works.

Chapter 1 – Self-Protection

Every person in this world is in one of three groups. One is either a predator, the prey, or a protector. Depending on circumstances, one can move between these three groups, but typically everyone has a primary group. Like a lion, a predator is born to hunt. They are always looking for the best opportunities to engage and take down their prey. Predators may hunt alone or in a group, either way, predators will hunt. Predators might use trickery, beauty, or deception to lure in its prey but regardless of how they do it, predators will hunt, and given a clear opportunity they will strike. If one has not noticed the main point, understand that predators will hunt for prey and if one is not careful, one can easily become the prey.

Then there is the prey. Like sheep, the prey has been so domesticated that they have all but lost the ability to defend themselves from predators. They require outside protection to keep them safe. Even when they see a predator attack, they freeze in place and fail to react. Some call this the bystander effect when an individual fails to act, assuming that someone else will do it. Regardless of what labels it is given, prey has the false assumption that their safety is someone else's responsibility. Even as children, we consider our personal safety the responsibility of our parents. While parents have the overall responsibility for a child's protection, one's immediate safety is still a personal responsibility regardless of age. Parents and guardians are not present 100% of the time. It is within these windows that predators will look to strike.

Finally, there are the protectors. Protectors are like the vast herds of the African plain such as the wildebeest. They know the predators are out there, they understand how predators operate, and they have learned to live with it despite the potential danger. When predators attack, protectors come together to provide mutual aid; not after but during the attack. Protectors are always looking out for predators and trying to minimize predators' opportunities whenever possible.

There will always be predators among us. Even among those reading this book, there are predators reading and looking for ways to subvert the techniques I outline. Do not be a predator. There will always be prey. One should strive never to be the prey. Prey will always abdicate responsibility for their own safety to someone else. In fact, there will be a group who read this book and refuse to do any of the exercises because they do not feel that it applies to them. An overinflated ego is one of the primary reasons that some become prey. They tend to entrust their safety to the very predators they wish to avoid. So common is this occurrence that our language contains the cliche' "A wolf in sheep's clothing." Meaning the best predators will go unnoticed right up until the moment they strike.

One should strive to be the protector. Protectors understand their role in keeping all others safe. The protector knows that they cannot give up their responsibility to be vigilant as it can bring harm to themselves and others. A person should study, train and practice to always be a protector.

Later in this book, we will discuss exercises and drills to improve one's protective skills. They are highlighted in several sections. Of all the information in this book, the drills will have the absolute greatest impact on one's immediate safety. Personalize them, make them fun, but most important of all do them!

Let us look at how to become a protector. We start by looking at self-protection as a pyramid. Self-protection starts with the five "D's," deter, detect, defuse, depart, and defend. Expanding one's understanding of each of these levels strengthens one's overall protective abilities. As the threat of violence increases, the number of options decreases, so it is important to learn and train to build the broadest base to one's pyramid as possible.

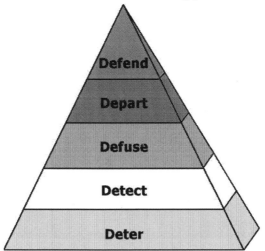

Deter

Self-Protection starts with deterrence. The definition of deterrence is "The action of discouraging an act or event through instilling doubt or fear of the consequences or outcome." While that is a textbook definition, my grandma would say, "An ounce of prevention is worth a pound of cure." Deterrence is that ounce of prevention. Most criminal and violent acts start with the predator or predators making a judgment call of the risks versus the rewards. If the risks and the consequences are low, but the gains are high, they will proceed. This evaluation is the motivation behind large-scale crimes like a home invasion, carjacking, and identity theft. While the rewards are different, this motivation can be found even in smaller scale acts such as bullying. With that in mind, one's best self-defense technique is doing everything it takes not to become the prey. Deterrence is a twenty-four hour a day task. A person should practice some act of deterrence either actively or passively all the time. Deterrence should not make one feel paranoid about the potential for crime and violence. However, one should not allow their regiment of deterrence to become so routine, that they are done without thought. There is always a need to evaluate the effectiveness of the techniques being used.

The scope of deterrence is vast. It should include simple things such as closing the garage door, locking the doors when at home, locking the car door when filling up the gas tank and most commonly putting away the smartphone while walking down the street. While these acts of deterrence may seem simple, do not dismiss them because these acts prevent crimes of opportunity. More involved measures can include alarm systems, home security cameras, and gates on the windows. Much of this is beyond the scope of this book. I recommend a family discussion along the lines of "What can we do to prevent the crime of..."?

While it seems frivolous, role-playing helps to flush out misconceptions of how things will play out in reality. Like all things one wishes to be good at, practice is required. Deterrence is no exception. One of the exercises I engage in constantly is outlined later as the **"I'm Billy Bad"** drill. The drill starts with the idea of what will a predator do? I restart this each time I enter a new location. I look at each place and decide how I would respond in the case of fire, robbery, or random attack. It has become so second nature that I find myself maintaining this level of awareness and vigilance even when it is not a conscious thought. A habit of active deterrence is what a person wants to develop to maximize the chances of being safe anywhere. In any situation, the objective is to work back down the personal protection pyramid to a level of constant deterrence.

Rings of Safety

Active deterrence should be looked at as colored safety rings. The outer most ring extends about 50 feet or 15 meters from one's person. This is the green zone. The middle zone extends about 25 feet or 8 meters. This is the yellow zone. Finally, within 10 feet or 2 meters is the red zone. The closer an individual is, the greater ones' level of awareness and deterrence should be. On the outer most region one should take notice of everything that is going on. If anything changes suddenly or seems out of the ordinary, one should focus in on it and evaluate it as a potential threat.

As people approach the yellow ring, one should be tracking everything and everyone. If anything changes, focus on it immediately determine why are they there and are they behaving suspiciously. Be ready to act if needed regardless of familiarity.

Finally, within the red ring, one should be observant of everyone. When people are this close, negative things can happen within a second or two. Within this range wallets can be lifted, purses snatched, and people grabbed. This range should be considered personal space. If someone is this close in proximity, the techniques learned from the **"Defensive Fence"** drill should come into play. In most cases, there is no threat, but being prepared is the ultimate goal.

Detect

Despite one's best efforts, no level of deterrence is 100% effective. When preventive measures have failed, it helps to be able to detect potential dangers and react before they become serious problems. By being aware of one's current surroundings and anything that is out of the ordinary, a person typically notices trouble before it starts. Recognizing a potential threat and doing what it takes to counter it is the quickest way to de-escalate any potential problem. Detection requires that one be imaginative, vigilant, and observant. For example, a backpack on the ground to most people is a backpack on the ground. However, on July 27th, 1996 during the Olympics in Atlanta, Richard Jewell, a security guard, spotted a green backpack under a park bench. He alerted the authorities and helped to move people away from the device. When the device exploded, it killed one person and injured over 100 others. Had it not been for Richard's diligence in looking for and detecting potential threats, this tragedy would have been substantially worse.

To be able to detect a threat, a person must think like a predator and imagine how they would be a threat. This reverse thinking on identifying where a threat may come from is an exercise similar to building muscles. The more one thinks like a predator, the easier it is to see potential problems. Without being paranoid, a constant awareness of what could go wrong, and the observation of people and events in the immediate area is an integral part of the personal self-protection process. Many may be uncomfortable with the idea of thinking like a predator, but knowing the predator mindset does not make you a predator nor does it draw predators near. The wildebeest know the tactics of the lion, but that does not make them a lion. It allows them to know when and where to be hyper-vigilant. The same is true for people. If a person knows where, when, and how an attack may come, it makes it easy to look for possible exits, and defensive positions. So the first step to detecting a problem is knowing what to look for and why.

The second step in detecting a threat is imagining the various ways an attack will start. This will allow one to recognize an attack as it begins and take steps to minimize it.

When training in my basement, affectionally known as the War Room, we often do the "**Abduction**" drill listed later in this book. As the name indicates, in this drill we simulate the student being abducted. The downside of this drill is the students know it's coming. In order to add some variety, I decided to catch the students by surprise.

As students arrived, I showed them down the stairs, allowing them to go first. While behind them, I put my safety goggles on, the indicator that I am no longer an instructor but a predator. I would then grab them at the bottom of the stairs and drag them from one room about 30 feet, the distance to a waiting van or into the woods.

Kelley was the first to arrive. She walked down the stairs ahead of me. Detecting that she might not be safe with me behind her, she quickly stepped down the stairs putting distance between herself and me. Darting into the game room; she looked for a clear field of view to face her would-be attacker. She went to the opposite side of the pool table and turned to face me. Seeing the glasses on my face, she laughed knowing that she had escaped a planned attack. Kelley had expanded her protective base enough to detect that she might not be safe, with me close behind saying nothing, so she took measures to deter any attempt to abduct her.

Detection in the real world is just that simple. You know the feeling one gets when the hairs raise on the back of the neck, that is the body saying something is wrong. Listen to it. My favorite personal experience was in the Times Square area of New York City. I was there for a trade show. It was early in the morning. I was standing outside of a little bistro waiting on my team. Since we were still setting up, I was dressed in warmup pants and had my wallet tucked in my waistband. Yes, it was clearly visible. Now, simple deterrence practices tell me that I should put my wallet up, but I did not. Doing a routine scan of the area, I noticed a guy approaching from well outside of my green zone. He caught my attention simply because his stare was fixed on me while everyone else seemed preoccupied with where they were going or what they were doing.

As he got closer into my yellow zone, I noticed that the angle of his approach had changed. He started walking directly toward me. I actively paid attention to him through my peripheral vision. The safest practice would have been to move my wallet and turn toward the approaching predator acknowledging that I was aware of his presence. But I did not. I was actually curious to see if he would be so bold as to confront me face-to-face. So, I did nothing until he entered my red zone. At that time, I turned toward him, stepped into a defensive stance, placed my hand on top of my wallet and simply looked at him with a classic, are you stupid expression and asked, "can I help you?"

The man stopped in his tracks and looked stunned. He asked if I knew why the delivery truck, which was parked right in front of me, was there. I assume that it was all he could think of at that moment. Without looking away, I said, " Hmm, I had not noticed it, but what I have noticed was the thousands of cops in town for the International Association of Chiefs of Police Convention!" Then looking sideways at a group of people wearing name tags, I made an educated guess, and greeted them with "Morning Chief." Even to my surprise about four different people looked my way and responded with some form of salutation. The would-be predator's face went white. Without missing a beat, I crossed my arms over my chest, still holding my wallet, reared back and said, "Yep, this would be a bad week to be a crook in Times Square!" The would-be predator quickly walked off without saying another word.

Technically, I cannot say that this individual was trying to take my wallet as he never made an active attempt, but I was able to detect someone acting suspiciously. I identified a potential target and took the steps needed to defuse a potential criminal situation by applying a great level of deterrence, which brings us to our next level of personal protection.

Defuse

After a threat has presented itself, it is essential that one makes every effort to defuse it. Understand that it is not always possible to defuse all conflicts or potentially violent acts. Defusing a conflict can be a difficult task. It requires excellent self-control and social awareness. Within seconds, one must be able to assess a predator's motivations and compile a list of potential outcomes, and as the victim, prepare a list of risk versus reward calculations. Every action taken to defuse any situation will have a consequence/reward regardless of the scenario. Take the following example:

In a holdup, a person can choose to give up valuables and hope the robbers will leave, try to talk them out of the act altogether, or fight and hopefully best the predator and prevent them from ever doing it again. No one can say what's the best action every time but staying calm and knowing one's options will lead to the best choice at that time. In all cases, be secure within oneself and try not to escalate the issue unless necessary.

The key to defusing a conflict is, first of all, remaining calm. Start by being calm and rational, hostility and escalating tension will never defuse a problem. Make no assumptions about what is going on. Second, observe the warning signs, taking notice of any changes in a person's personality, actions or any rise in predatory communications. Often this kind of communication will include rudeness, sarcasm and dismissive comments. Third, one should talk and listen. Engage in a measured dialogue and try to gain a level of understanding. Even in the midst of fear and anger, maintain a pleasant disposition. Someone must be willing to take the high road and work to understand and resolve any potential conflict. It is not about being right or wrong but reaching a resolution to the problem. Listen closely to what is said and what is not said. Quite often unspoken comments are as important as what is said. Those unspoken comments can indicate a simple miscommunication. Many conflicts can be defused with honest dialogue and a simple understanding of the other's point of view. During a conversation, I will frequently pause and say, "Now let me tell you what I think you told me." Doing this shows that I am listening and allows them to correct my understanding of their point of view. Many times people who feel pushed to violence do not have a viable way of communicating their feelings. Taking steps to understand another can be the pressure valve needed to prevent large-scale violence in the future.

Finally, understand that defusing a potentially violent conflict is not always a solitary act. If one notices a classmate constantly talking about hurting another student, or shooting up the school, do not try to handle this alone. Also, in the workplace, if it is determined that a co-worker's entire demeanor has changed, or that person has become short-tempered and distracted, this is the time in which one should seek additional help. There is no need to panic. Quite often an understanding ear or a show of strength is all that is needed to defuse a violent or criminal situation.

Depart

If a conflict begins to go south, take any opportunity that presents itself to depart the area! If one walks away or runs, distance is often the best way to remove oneself from the situation. Evaluate the situation and back away if needed. There are many times when turning one's back is not a viable option. At this point, people should realize, they are desperately short of other options and violence may be imminent. Even if one departs, there is no guarantee that the predator will not give chase, or that it will not lead to an even more dire confrontation later. Regardless, make this decision to depart from a position of knowledge, and not fear. The act of withdrawing from conflict should play to one's strengths. If leaving the location of the conflict will make you more vulnerable then do not go. An example of this occurred here in Atlanta. Five predators attacked a homeless marine. He chose to depart the assault, running through the neighborhood calling for help. Finally, he was chased down cornered and forced to defend himself. Pulling a knife, he fought back killing one and hospitalizing three others. He said he ran to avoid having to hurt anyone, but failing to get help with his screams, he had to defend himself. After neutralizing the attack, he ran to the nearest house to ask for police assistance.

Always look to depart when violence is imminent. In the example of the homeless marine, Yelling for help was an attempt to defuse the problem. However, because of the bystander effect, no one wanted to get involved. Thus, the marine was forced to resort to violence to protect his life.

Defend

Finally, if necessary, defend oneself when left with no other choice. Before the first punch, one should know why they are fighting and understand how far they are willing to go. If fighting a bully, then putting them to the ground may be enough. If fighting an unknown predator, it may require more, maybe even taking a life. Intentional or not, death is always a potential outcome one must know and think about long before ever considering defending oneself. This is a great time to pause and ask "what should I do if?" Under what conditions will I fight? Under what circumstances will I stop fighting? Under what circumstances will I knowingly try to take a life? These questions are not just for the adult, but children as well. I recall a 12-year old girl shooting a home invader while she was home alone. She was on the phone with her mother when the home invader entered the house. With the instructions of her mother, she grabbed the family gun and hid in the closet. As the predator heard her whispering in the closet, he started opening the door when she decided to shoot. She had full knowledge and understanding of what she was doing when she pulled the trigger. A conversation that should take place between parents, children, or families is what I will do when? It is hard to fight back with the appropriate amount of force if one has never considered the possibilities. Now, I am not suggesting that twelve-year-olds be told to pull a gun at the first sign of trouble, but there needs to be a discussion of what is acceptable in one's family. Talk to your parents and set expectations.

For children who are most often dealing with the local bully, or a similar situation, I suggest the same rules that I used to raise my boys which are as follows:

- Under no conditions should one start, instigate, or facilitate a fight.
- Do your best to avoid a fight.
- If one must fight, do not throw the first punch but land the first and last punch!
- Fight to win. Win decisively to prevent any future fights. The confrontation is not over until the predator will not or cannot continue.

Understand I was an involved father. I was involved with the school and had a relationship with the principals. While this was my method, I recommend that parents reach out to school officials to develop two-way open communications regarding expectations for individual safety and behavior at school.

Yes, that sounds very "**adult-ish**." In short, kids, if there is a problem at school, get your parents involved early. You need them to advocate for you. There needs to be a documented record of what was going on so that they may defend you if you are forced to fight.

As my boys grew, my requirements changed. They were required to tolerate a bit more than most kids as they have been training with me since they could walk. When dealing with an in-school bully, they were instructed to do as follows:

- The first time a bully strikes them, instruct the bully to stop and inform the teacher.
- The second time they are to instruct the bully to stop, inform the teacher and tell me about it. I will discuss this with the school administration.
- The third time they are to tell the bully to stop, inform the teacher and me. I will meet with the school's principal to demand a resolution to the problem.
- The fourth time they are attacked my boys were to fight back. The effort should make the statement, "I will not be a victim."

While this may sound harsh, if one did not initiate the fight, winning convincingly, ends that conflict and may serve to prevent future one-on-one physical conflicts.

This is where parents and documentation come into play. Some schools have rules which say that both students in a fight must be punished. As a parent, I would demand that the staff tell me how else was my child to protect himself if I can document that they have been a victim of repeated attacks. Parents need to be willing and able to stand up for their kids. Fortunately, I never had to put this to the test within the school. My boys were not the type of kids bullies wanted to pick on.

As college students and young adults, one should be far too old for schoolyard fights. When two adults decide to allow their egos to get in the way and both sides refuse to back down, that is not self-defense or self-protection. That is just stupidity. The only time an adult should choose to fight is to protect one's self or others.

With young adults, the problem of physical conflict is that the stakes are much higher. One never knows how far a predator is willing to go when escalating a conflict to a fight. Will it end with just a fist fight? Will they pull a weapon? Are they looking to kill someone? If an adult predator refuses to de-escalate a conflict, there is no way of knowing how far they are willing to go. Knowing this, young adults should not fight unless it is absolutely necessary, and they should not stop until the predator cannot continue. A predator should be disabled sufficiently to allow one to put a substantial distance between them self and the predator. While this might seem extreme, one must consider the alternatives. If a person has tried everything possible to avoid violence and is unsuccessful, then there are only two choices. One can choose to be prey or a protector. There are no other options.

Chapter 2 – Motives for Violence

One of my favorite questions ever is why? As I child I am sure I drove my father insane asking why to everything. It made no sense to me to do anything unless I understood why. To this day I still ask why. Why do people commit crimes, why do people choose violence? That is where I started when writing this book. It took less than 30 minutes of online research to determine that I was asking the wrong question. My search resulted in over educated contrived answers like overpopulation, poverty, and regionalism.

I thought to myself, "Really? um, NO". While somewhere down the line I am sure those answers may be relevant. I seriously doubt that an individual pointing a gun in my face is looking to solve the problem of overpopulation or world poverty. Either the people writing the articles are so educated that they cannot answer a simple question or I was asking the wrong question. So, I started with a new question. My new question was why do individuals resort to crime and violence? This is important to understand if we wish to be safe. An understanding of the cause can often lead to understanding how to preempt it so that it does not happen again. There are only a few fundamental reasons for violence all of which we will discuss here. Also, know that mental defects or drug addiction can significantly alter a predator's perception of reality and impair their ability to reason and violence is the one action that requires no real thought.

After understanding the cause of violence, we refer back to the personal protection pyramid where deterrence is the largest of all levels. We want to make sure that we do what it takes to eliminate the threats and temptations of crime and violence by limiting the opportunities predators have.

Deterrence is an ever-changing environment. One must adapt to new tactics and new technologies as we incorporate those technologies into our daily life. We must realize that the things that make life easier and keep us connected to our friends can be the same tools that predators use to find their prey. Facebook, Instagram, and social media are the latest tools predators use to identify prey, but it is not limited to just these platforms. We walk around paying attention to our smartphone with Beats headphones completely oblivious to the world. What we did not notice is the stranger who was admiring those headphones and eyeing the smartphone as well. In this section, I will outline some the techniques needed to deter particular types of crimes but under no circumstances is this a complete list. That is where the "**What Would You Do If**" drills come into play. Examine these techniques to see how they can be expanded and again make the games fit individual lifestyles.

Money & Assets

There is the tired old cliché, "Money is the root of all evil," I disagree. A better statement would be, "The lust for what one can do with money is the root of evil." While not quite as catchy or succinct, this statement is more accurate. People do not steal one's money to look at it. They want what they can do and acquire with money. Money is the physical embodiment of power and control. Predators without it will go to great lengths to get it. Far more surprising is how far some are willing to go to get just a little. While I may not think fifty dollars is worth hurting someone over, there are those who have been seriously hurt or killed for less.

This envy, jealousy, and greed are motives as old as humanity. Many robberies have a threat of violence, but most thieves prefer not to resort to violence and will gladly depart with the property. Some robberies use violence as a way to cover the criminal's escape. An example would be a burglar who happens to be in the residence when the homeowner returns. They may use violence not so much to complete the robbery but as a way to hide their crime from the police.

In the next chapter, we will discuss some of the common-sense deterrence methods, but this cannot be said too often. The most basic method of deterring physical robberies can be summed up as being aware of one's surroundings and limiting the amount of personal information published. Knowing what is going on in one's environment is not difficult, it does require a person to put down the technology and focus on what is going on around them. Take notice of the people. Is there anyone paying undue attention to your comings and goings? For example, when you stop to fill your car with gas are the windows up, and the doors locked? On social media how much personal information is available? Is the amount of your Christmas bonus listed? These seem to be obvious, but we often get into such a rush that we ignore the simple things. Predators are usually not the most intelligent people on the planet. They are looking for crimes of opportunity. If a thief can punch someone in the head, take their property, and flee, that is a quick and easy score. In the equation of risk versus reward, this qualifies as low risk and easy reward.

A bit more sophisticated robbery can be the home burglary or the home invasion. Often, predators try to make sure no one is home by knocking on the door and walking around the house. If no one answers, the thieves will proceed to make entry. When it comes to this home burglaries, not answering the door can be detrimental as it indicates to potential thieves no one is home. The home invasion, on the other hand, is intended to take place while someone is home. Regardless of burglary or home invasion, the preparation is the same. Modern technology can easily be the first step in preparing a deterrence. Equipment such as a video doorbell and exterior cameras can be a powerful deterrent as the predator knows their every action is recorded. A predator who is looking to avoid a video system must conceal their face, a clear indication to the homeowner that the person at their door is up to no good. If one has a video doorbell, the homeowner can address someone at the door regardless of their location.

While this is a powerful deterrent, it does not prevent a predator from making entry into the home, particularly if that was their initial intention. A second powerful deterrent is a home alarm system. The siren of an alarm system is designed to attract attention, but one must have neighbors who are protectors and not prey. The loudest alarm in the world is of no value if the neighbors do not respond or call the police. The greatest deterrent, to robberies, is a community of protectors.

Criminal Exploitation

In the realm of crimes for money and assets, sex and drugs are the biggest criminal enterprises and should never be overlooked. These criminal business ventures pose various threats to individual safety. We will expand on each of these enterprises and how they affect young people.

Drugs and Violence

Whether illicit or prescribed drugs have probably touched every family in this country in some way or another. Drug trafficking is the number one criminal enterprise in the world, and young people are front and center in the industry. Drugs, be it marijuana, opioids, meth, you name it, they are in the schools, neighborhoods, and homes. If it can alter one's current state of mind or physical state, people will abuse it. For most people, their interaction with the drug world is a choice, albeit a bad choice but a choice none the less. If a person wants to avoid the potential violence of the drug world, do not take, sell or get involved in drugs in any manner. There, spoken just like a public service announcement or health teacher.

Not to take the subject lightly, drug trafficking is a violent world. The drug trade is not regulated, there are no quality standards, and by definition, everyone in the trade is a criminal. The very nature of the business being illegal attracts people who do not care about laws, including laws against violence. Those willing to buy and sell drugs are often willing to rob, steal, assault, and if need be, kill for money or a simple fix. Since drug transactions are not done in well-lit places like banks, the drug trade lends itself to opportunistic violence. In an industry run by criminals, there is no trust.

While much debate occurs around the legalization of cannabis or marijuana, it remains illegal in many states. People are often hurt, injured and even killed in the act of selling and buying Marijuana.

Other drugs like meth, and heroin, lead to violence because of their effects on the mind and body. The chemicals in these drugs change the body causing physical dependency to such a state that one will do just about anything to get more drugs including, robbery and murder. In short, drugs are highly addictive. Following that initial euphoria, one is always chasing that high. And as many recovering addicts will say, you will never get as high as that first high. Whether self-medicating, experimenting, or looking to make a quick buck, your high school health teacher was right. Nothing good will come from drugs. I am not making moral judgments in this book, but if Marijuana is not legal in your state, stay away from it and all other illegal drugs.

Human Trafficking

This particular section of the book may be upsetting to the reader as it is to me the author. I have been blessed with two great boys. But I always wanted a girl. Throughout the years several wonderful young ladies have come into my life along with two great Goddaughters. They grew up alongside my boys and, to them, I have been like a second father. As I did the research for this section, I would find myself thinking of them and getting upset just writing my notes. I understand why God chose not to give me a little girl!

I almost want to apologize for adding this section as it is incredibly heavy for a young audience. In fact, this section was omitted from the first draft of this book. But as I talked to young men and women, some not even teenagers yet, they are far more knowledgeable on the subject than I recall being at their age. Ultimately, it was kids who ensured me that this section was as important if not more than a discussion on bullying.

As I understood the scope of this hidden problem, I started to think about the audience for this book. My intention was high school and college. Although the subject matter is a bit heavy for middle schoolers, they are the prime target for traffickers. So, with this fact in mind, I decided to include them in my target audience as they are among the most likely to be victims.

Let us begin with a definition and a few facts. First, what is Human trafficking? Human Trafficking is defined as the action or practice of illegally transporting people from one area to another, typically for the purposes of forced labor or commercial sexual exploitation. Human trafficking has surpassed illegal arms sales and is currently second only to drug trafficking. Unlike drugs, humans can be sold over and over again. Despite how widespread trafficking is we hardly ever hear about it on the nightly news. Quite often we hear of this happening in other countries or other cultures. We even see these acts as backdrops to Hollywood movies like **Taken and The Equalizer.**

While such events seem far removed from our day to day lives, make no mistake, human trafficking is alive and well everywhere in the USA. While we think of trafficking as the domain of the seedy underworld of the mob, parents that offer their son or daughter as payment for drugs in exchange for money or something else are engaged in trafficking. That is a dirty little secret that happens far too frequently. I worked with a young lady who informed me that she lost her virginity when her mother sold her, for two months' rent, to a man her mother was dating.

Human traffickers have only one purpose, and that is to make money with people as their product. Sex is the most common industry that trafficked individuals find themselves engaged in. According to some estimates, 80% of trafficked individuals are involved in the sex trade for the purpose of prostitution or pornography. That leaves 20% who are used in forced servitude. I.E., Slavery. The average age of a girl entering the sex trade is 11-14 years old. Many are runaways who were sexually abused prior. Additionally, many victims are from other countries, looking to cash in on the promise of a better life in the United States or having been sold to a trafficker by a family member.

While the idea of being sold by a family member may be shocking, do understand in many parts of the world girls have little value. Moreover, in countries where the number of children one can have is limited, getting rid of a daughter to make room for a son is highly desirable.

If you do not truly understand the impact of sex trafficking, I give you this statement from Ludwig "Tarzan" Fainberg, a convicted trafficker. According to Fainberg, "You can buy a woman for $10,000 and make your money back in a week if she is pretty and young. Then everything else is profit." Unlike most other criminal enterprises, human trafficking is a trade that has women making up a significant number of victims at 80%. On the other hand, women also make up a large number of traffickers. Traffickers use the phrase "Use a slave to catch a slave." A teen girl who is cold and hungry is more likely to trust a nurturing woman or another young girl who is offering her a good meal and a warm place to sleep. Once a trusting victim walks into the predator's house, it is far too late for the unsuspecting prey.

Trafficking tends to target the most vulnerable in society, runaways, the LGBT community, abandoned and forgotten youth, and immigrants. Statistics show that teens are contacted by traffickers within 48 hours once the teen runs away from home and is on the streets. With limited funds and resources, most runaways are confronted with the idea of survival sex soon after leaving home.

However, do not assume that those living in suburbia and middle-class America are immune. Quite often young people who are sexually abused at home will find themselves in the middle of a nightmare when they fall victim to a charismatic older man who shows interest and concern for them. Young people who have already been victims tend to be the easiest to victimize. For them, it is extremely difficult to tell the difference between an adult that cares and one who is looking to exploit.

Human trafficking is not just a problem for the individual being trafficked. It is a plague within our society. Those who identify themselves as being at risk need to seek groups that can help them. It is not easy, as they have been conditioned not to trust others. Talking too much will often cause them to incur severe punishment from their traffickers. This is an extremely hard cycle to break, but as it is a community problem, it also takes the community to deter it. Those groups that wish to help need to be more visible and unified and nosey! The most vulnerable among us will not reach out unless they are 99% sure that they will be safer than they are now, and they do not wish to leave the devil they know for the hell they do not.

Adults, including Young adults, should get to know people they interact with and learn to identify people in crisis. Youth and young adults should know the techniques to vet people and ensure that any persons they are dealing with are also above board. It is important that even the most vulnerable be able to distinguish a protector from the most skillful predator.

Power & Control

The desire for power, control, status, and dominance often leads to violence, as it is the motivation behind bullying, domestic violence, stalkers, and hate crimes. This type of person often thinks violence is an acceptable method of gaining power, popularity, or control. They often use a group's fear to exert control over them.

Power and control crimes are difficult to deter and defuse because as a victim one is not perceived of as an equal. Thus, not entitled to the same quality of treatment as others. Quite often white supremacists refer to blacks as apes, monkeys or some other animal. Gays and Lesbians are called queers, freaks, fagots, and dikes. Similarly, one of the worst cases of genocides in modern memory, Adolf Hitler considered the Jews to be sub-human, to the point that killing them all was considered a viable solution.

While the Holocaust is a particularly extreme example, the entire rise of the Nazi party is a clear-cut example of people using violence for the purpose of power and control. I will address each type of power and control crime and give suggestions on how to deter and defuse them. Remember, this is in no way a complete list of options, nor can it ever be. The intent is to start a thought process that extends into one's own daily life. Before resorting to violence, seek out authorities and reach out for help early! These situations never resolve themselves. The more one pushes back, those looking to exert power and control often push harder. It may require something that the predator cannot control to bring an end to their behavior. If this situation turns violent, the first option should always be to depart if possible. If there is no other option left but to fight, it is imperative that one fights not only to win this single fight but to prevent future fights as well. The predator should know that under no circumstances will they ever win. Keep in mind that under these conditions some seeking control can seek the ultimate end. i.e., "If I cannot have you no one can." Never underestimate the levels to which these types will resort. Make it a priority to determine the motives of such people as it is the only effective way to devise a method to end their behavior. Reach out for help early, because when this situation gets serious, it will get serious quickly.

Women and girls often convince themselves, "I can handle them." Please understand, one can never control a predator's actions; only how you react to them. Do not make the mistake of thinking "I have this under control" as predators will continue to escalate their actions until they feel they are in control. With this said, let us discuss some specific types of control crimes and how to address them.

The Stalker

Let us first discuss stalking. Being a victim of a stalker can be paralyzing in its effect. It tends to reach into every aspect of a victim's life, altering their very perception of the world. One woman said it felt like being raped in slow motion. I cannot imagine how violated she must have felt, but if her description is accurate, there are few things worse. Stalkers tend to claim that they are in love, and the victim needs to realize they love the stalker as well. In reality, it is all about control and possession. A stalker will not stop unless stopped. As a victim, it is almost impossible to stop a stalker. In the mind of a stalker, the victim is a possession, like a pet, and not a person; therefore, what the victim wants does not matter. In the stalker's mind, they are justified in their actions because it is what they want and believes they need. Stalkers tend to have a rather self-centered view of the world.

I encountered a stalker almost a year after his girlfriend broke up with him. Out of the clear blue, he showed up on her college campus some two hours away from his home. He kept repeating "I just want my girlfriend back." Not once did he use her name. With stalkers, it is almost always about what the stalker wants, feels or believes they need. It is most important to understand to end the actions of a stalker one must almost always get outside help. I understand people do not want others in their business, but privacy is not worth getting hurt over.

Stalkers, in general, are an odd breed. It is hard to say what in particular will make a person go from "hello how are you" to "I cannot live without you."

Deterring stalkers is almost impossible because their triggers cannot be readily identified, and when one does, it is often too late. First thing in dealing with a stalker is to recognize that you need help and things have gotten out of control. The graveyard is full of people who thought they had it under control. Remember, one is not viewed as a person but as an object or possession. Bring in outside help quickly. Let friends, family, and coworkers know what is going on. In some situations not only is the victim in danger but those closest to them can be in danger as well. At the first hint of intimidation or expression of violence, get the police involved. Do not dismiss the situation by thinking it will all just go away if ignored; it will not. Ignoring it only makes it worse because the stalker needs the interaction. Good or bad a stalker wants the victim to acknowledge and interact with them. Negative interaction is better than no interaction at all. At least that way the victim is paying attention to them.

The ordeal of being stalked may end simply by having someone else talk some sense into the stalker, or it may require getting law enforcement involved and taking out a restraining order. Be mindful, that bringing in outside help may also trigger an escalation in the stalker's mind. In some cases, a restraining order is just a challenge, and the stalker will be emboldened to show that a simple piece of paper will not stop them. If these steps to stop a stalker fail, be prepared for an elevated level of hostility. Extreme cases may require deadly force if the stalker decides they would rather hurt you than let you go. If this ever happens, be prepared both mentally and physically. Ask the question "What Would I do If?" If violence erupts, what are you prepared to do. Do not be afraid to envision the best and worse possible outcomes.

For those under the age of 18 who have to attend school with their stalkers, talk to parents. Be honest and factual. Bring this to their attention and let them know all the details, the good, bad, and ugly. Do not allow parents to downplay one's fears as being melodramatic. Yes, teens have a flair for the dramatic, but in some cases, emotionally immature teens are the most volatile and violent predators as they have not yet learned to handle the emotional pain of rejection.

The Bully

Before we deal with bullying, let us first define what bullying is and is not. In the modern context, the term bully is applied to anyone whose opinion differs from our own, and they refuse to alter their view. That is not bullying, but when the tactics used to force someone to change their views include such things as belittling, name-calling, and public shaming as a manner to control someone else's views that is classic bullying. For our discussion in this book, a bully is a person who uses verbal abuse, intimidation or physical violence to gain a sense of power or control over someone else.

Bullying is a form of dominance behavior. Its foundations are in one's desire to perceive themselves as powerful, in control, and a winner. While it appears to be hateful, the source of bullying usually has nothing to do with hate at all. Domestic violence is a common form of bullying, and it is against people that the bully often claims to love. A person bullies another as a way to deal with their insecurities. Bullies tend to need outside validation of how they would like others to see them, so they often act out with an entourage of associates who serve to feed their ego and encourage their actions providing a sense of empowerment.

Bullies often lack the social skills needed to deal with their feelings of weakness and inadequacy, their inability to make friends and influence others as well as the coping mechanisms to deal with undesirable life changes. For these reasons, bullies use threats, intimidation, and violence to either feed their ego, vent their frustration, or control their environment.

In some cases, bullies are projecting onto others behaviors and treatments that they have received such as a prior role as a victim of a bully themselves or the product of a troubled home life. If one does not address bullying within their environment, it will often escalate as it is a primal behavior requiring little skill.

Preventing bullying is also difficult, as the victim usually has little to nothing to do with why the bully has picked them as a target. It is vital that as the victim of a bully one understands that it is not their fault. Bullies will typically pick on a unique characteristic one has and make fun of it. Physical size is a typical characteristic used by bullies to select their targets, as picking on someone smaller is often safer for the bully. Something as simple as skin color, the clothes one wears, a person's weight or anything detected as a weakness or difference will be exploited. Social status, family income, disabilities, and in general, any other difference is often exploited by bullies to identify and isolate their target.

Bullying is not limited to a schoolyard activity, it sometimes also takes place in homes and the workplace. One should deal with this as early as possible. While many people do not like being seen as a snitch or tattletale the best and the first course of action a person can take is to get outside help, if a person is bullied at school, then that would require involving a teacher, or school administrators. If one has to deal with a bully at work, it will require getting management or human resources involved. Finally, if one's bully is at home then get parents involved. In our modern environment, one of the constant concerns with confronting bullies and others is the fact that many do not seem to have limits. What used to be fistfights in the old days, can quickly escalate to guns and knives now. For this reason, even at the middle school level, one should be concerned enough to involve those with greater knowledge. In the case of the schoolyard or neighborhood bully, one may have a few other alternatives before the bullying turns physical.

Quite often a bully is looking for a reaction. They feel powerful when making others feel weak. They will often use teasing or name calling to get a reaction. Simply not reacting in the manner in which they expect is often an easy way to counter a bully. Sometimes, it is best simply to walk away or not respond. Other times, countering with a quick wit will also make some bullies think twice. Often, they are not looking for a battle of wits. However, be forewarned that antagonizing a bully may very well provoke them to violence to save face.

Finally, the last set of actions is to call the bully out. Take a stand picking a time and place that is the most advantageous and confront the bully. A bully that is not looking for a fight will back down unless he is just so embarrassed that he will fight to save face like a mouse backed into a corner. Be careful not to use the confrontation to turn from bullied into being the bully. If one's bully decides to pursue a physical fight, then fight using the techniques listed later in this book, strike first, fast, furious, forward, and preferably to the face. Fight to win this fight and the next fight as well. Make it known that they will not win any future fight. As always, be prepared for an act of retaliation. The majority of times there is no retaliation, but one must consider it to be within the realm of possibilities.

Domestic Violence

Almost every family has some degree of exposure to domestic violence, if not in one's immediate family, then in a close relative or friend's family. It is a dirty little secret that people often do not talk about but, domestic violence affects everyone in the family. It can be one spouse beating on the other or an adult beating on the children. It is far too often that we hear the results of this type of abuse on the nightly news resulting in a dead child. Young people including college students are particularly vulnerable to this type of behavior as everything in their world depends on what parents are willing to provide. Part of their fear is not to make their situation worse than it currently is, but the fact is children, young people and young adults who are abused need to speak up. Even though the abuser may be a parent, one must seek help.

Adults who are willing need first to learn how to help. Just confronting the abuser will make it worse, adults who are willing to intercede need to provide a plan which may require getting that person out of their environment. However it is done, adults, including young adults, should learn to identify the signs of abuse and offer to intercede if needed. Be cautious not to force yourself into someone else's domestic issues. Seek professional help such as a school counselor. Alerting someone else to the problem can draw much needed attention. Most important, is that you be there to provide support for the victim when the time comes.

Finally, understand that domestic violence is not just between adults and children. Many teens and young adults have relationships with abusive partners. It is very common as people have not matured to handle their emotions yet. When I was in high school, I overheard one young lady tell another that your boyfriend does not love you if he does not hit you. I am sorry but, under no condition, should a boyfriend, girlfriend or a partner feel that they have the right to inflict physical, mental, or emotional abuse. Moreover, one is absolutely insane if one thinks that it is love. That is not love or affection. Secondly, do not believe the lie of "I will never do it again." Unless professional help is rendered, then nothing has changed. Seek to end any relationship that gets abusive immediately, and mentally know that a person who has wishes to control with physical violence may also resort to stalking. Any breakup with this type of person should be clear with no waffling back and forth when the relationship is over. Over should be over, done, finished, the end. There is no need to be rude and ugly about it, but be decisive with the understanding that there is no going back. Once abusive partners see that they can come back once, they will assume that they can do it again and again. Abusers need help before they change, and as the victim of the violence, you are viewed as a possession and not an equal.

Hate Crimes / Ideology

Hate crimes are all about the perpetrator's fears or inadequacies. It comes from their inability to control what they do not understand. The most common perpetrators of hate crimes are individuals who are looking to feel powerful or dominant, so they find an easy victim that they perceive as weak and vulnerable. Hate crimes are like bullying taken to the extreme. Attackers do not see their victims as human or equal, and often blame them for their perceived problems. One can think of this as a tribal mentality. Attackers view their victims as belonging to another group that is sub-human or inherently evil. As hate crimes cover a variety of motivations, we need to break them down into two types to evaluate how to deal with them. We will class them as hatemongers, and ideologues.

The Hatemonger

Hate is a potent force. It can lead a person to attack a church like the shooter in Charleston or the attacker at the Tree of Life synagogue in Philadelphia. The motivation of the hatemonger has little to nothing to do with the individual target and often catches the victims unawares.

Hate mongers would include any group of people who are utterly intolerant of other groups for one reason or another. Groups such as the KKK and the Arian Brotherhood qualify as hatemongers. Anyone who is willing to resort to violence because they do not like another's race, religion, sexual orientation or political views is a hatemonger. This type of person can only be deterred with overwhelming force; not overwhelming violence. These people do not see different groups as equals. Instead, the despised group's very existence is a threat to them. Such a narrow tolerance of others eliminates all possibilities of meaningful discussion. The way to stop or deter hatemongers is to get law enforcement involved or be prepared to defend oneself directly but lawfully.

The Ideologue

Ideologues, function very similar to hatemongers. An Ideologue is someone who is committed to a particular way of thinking and is unable or unwilling to change. Such is the mindset of political extremist and religious radicals. In the current political environment groups like Antifa believe that violence is acceptable to shut down the speech of those they oppose. Islamic radicals blame the west for interfering in their countries and oppressing their people. Right or wrong, they are eager to avenge their oppression by harming people who do not agree with their religious views. Again, there is no way to change their minds or negotiate. Be prepared to defend oneself or get law enforcement involved. In many cases, both may be needed.

Revenge

Revenge crimes are another form of control crime used to retaliate for a loss, humiliation or perceived injustice. Some use Intimidation, threats, physical assaults and even rape as methods of getting revenge. Far too often we see this with former and cheating lovers. Revenge is often the motive given by young offenders who feel that someone has disrespected them.

Deterring a revenge related crime requires an understanding and a sensitivity to the person that feels slighted. Revenge is one crime that has a definite trigger. There is always an event or act that serves as a trigger in this kind of crime. If one is a subject of a potential revenge attack, one should be aware of the predator's trigger. Typical triggers are often life-changing events and their anniversaries. While often an honest apology or talk with the offended party can stop the escalation, there are times when the offended person's rage is unstoppable. When this happens, there is nothing that can be done to prevent them from blowing up. Recognize this and become vigilant and make sure you are prepared to deal with an outraged individual.

Sexual Assaults

As a society, we are currently in flux about acceptable and unacceptable sexual contact. It depends on who you ask. While a consensual sexual encounter should not require a signed contract in triplicate, I do believe it should require some form of affirmative consent. For now, I will let others debate what is and is not acceptable. Here, we are going to use a legalistic definition for sexual assault. Rape is now defined by the Department of Justice as: "The penetration, no matter how slight, of the vagina or anus with any body part or object, or oral penetration of a sex organ of another person, without the consent of the victim." With that definition, understand that anyone can rape anyone else. A man can rape a woman or another man, and a woman can rape a man or another woman. Additionally, we will include sexual groping in this discussion of sexual assaults. For the sake of this book, we will consider sexual assault to be any unwanted or underage sexual contact.

While some predators confuse their sexual desires for love, sex crimes come from a place of control and hate! Sexual assaults, come in various forms and from multiple sources, and while boys and men tend to think they are immune to such, they are the most unprepared to be a victim of sexual assault when it happens, but the numbers show that boys are often victims as well.

In researching sexual assaults, there are numbers and statistics enough to make the mind go numb, each telling a story of who did what to whom and when. Most of them mean nothing, but others are significant. I made it a point to discard the statistics that failed to shed light on issues of safety and kept the rest. So, with all the numbers simplified allow me to point out the statistics that are crucially important.

- 20% of all girls and 8% of all boys are sexually assaulted by their 18th birthday.
- 54% of all sexual assault victims are between 18 and 34 years old
- 5% of all sexual Assaults occur in women under the age of 12.
- Ages 12-34 are the highest risk years of rape and sexual assault.
- Most victims know their attacker. Only about 7% of the time are the victims unknown.

Allow those numbers to sink in for just a moment. Notice the first two statistics. They are the most troubling. The first statistic of 20% means that one out of every five has either been sexually assaulted or will be before they are eighteen. I was in church shortly after I came across this statistic. I made it a point to look at the faces of the little girls as they exited for children's church. I pictured every fifth one as a victim. I realized regardless of which numbers one used, if accepted that many sex crimes go unreported, we cannot help but accept that we know many young people are forced to deal with their own personal hell at the hands of a family friend, family member, or acquaintance. It makes this section of the book vitally important and an area to discuss with young people.

Parents, one of the most effective measures you can use to increase your child's awareness is to share your personal experiences. For instance, if you have been a victim of a sexual assault, find a way to share this experience with your child. Although you may find this recommendation embarrassing and painful to share, sharing it may save your child from such a horrific experience.

Coaches, tutors, and mentors, if you are true in your desire to help, nurture, and prepare children, invite them to talk to you if they need a person to listen. Volunteer to intercede on their behalf if they need help talking to their parents. Become a knowledge source for places and people they may turn to for help.

Sexual crimes are committed through physical violence, overwhelming force, coercion, and sexual grooming. Note that I have separated this from human trafficking. While that too is a sexual act, trafficking is more of a criminal business enterprise. These sex crimes are more for control and gratification.

Violent Sexual Assault

A violent sexual assault is one in which the desire to cause physical harm is either more or equally as important to the predator as the actual sexual assault. This is what people think of when they hear the term "rapist." They also think of the perpetrator as being some night creeper who breaks into a house in the middle of the night with the intent to rape. This type of stranger on strange crime happens, but only 7% of rapes are stranger on stranger, and an additional 8% of rapes are by casual acquaintances. When these types of assaults do happen, the motive is often hatred or a mental defect. The physical act of rape is an additional tool to add to the victim's fear and humiliation.

Predators use any number of criteria to select their victims. Often they will pick victims that resemble certain people in their past that trigger hostile memories. They may also strike based on opportunity. In the predator's mind, they have done the risk versus reward calculations and have decided that a particular victim or opportunity provides a low risk of getting caught.

Within this group of "stranger on stranger" rapist, is the sexual sadist. A sadist is someone who receives sexual gratification from causing pain and suffering. Notable sadistic rapist/killers include Dennis Raider (BTK), John Wayne Gacy, and Ted Bundy. These are a particularly dangerous type of predator, as they refine their technique after each attack like a tradesman honing his craft. They are especially skilled in locating vulnerable people. As one never knows when they will encounter such an individual, it is extremely important to use the techniques of deterrence and to refine them as you learn more about how predators operate.

Good practices of basic deterrence will help one avoid becoming a victim of this particular form of sexual attacks. Ted Bundy would find the doors of college coeds unlocked, while Gacy would lure young men back to his house. Many times the stranger or casual acquaintance is quite personable and will persuade the person to lower their guard. To remain safe, be diligent and maintain the principles of personal protection around strangers, friends, and acquaintances at all times.

Forcible Rape

For the sake of motive, I label forcible rape as different from violent rape in that the sexual act is the primary goal. A victim's compliance can be gained using force and violence. While I separate forcible rape from violent sexual assaults, one act is by no means less traumatic than the other. I only separate these two types of sexual assaults because of the motivations behind the actions. A violent rape has every intention of causing pain or death as part of the crime. With forcible rape, violence, injury or death are actions taken as a result of forcing compliance.

Sexual gratification as a result of impulsive or obsessive lust is often a motivation behind forcible rape. Forcible rape can also be a tool for dominance and control, as well as revenge. Predators in these attacks are not seeking to hurt their victims. The predator is looking for a sexual release regardless of the willingness of their victim. Physical injury results because the victim wishes not to participate. This type of sexual assault is almost always performed by someone the victim knows even if it is just a casual acquaintance.

Sexual Coercion

Not all sexual assaults are physically violent or forceful, but that does not stop it from being an assault, or a crime. Coercion is when one uses pressure, fear, intimidation, alcohol or drugs, to force one to have sexual contact against their will. A simple example of this would be a predator who is substantially larger barring their victim from leaving and repeatedly demanding sex. While there is no direct threat of violence, the victim is being held or restrained against their will. Sexual coercion can also be something like refusing to return car keys until some sexual favor is performed. In any case, the victim is not providing freely formed consent.

Again, an ounce of deterrence can help minimize the risk of sexual coercion. While not everyone is a predator, be mindful not to be alone with someone new to your inner circle. If Bob, is a friend of my best friend, that does not make him a friend of mine, nor does it make him trustworthy.

Be mindful while drinking, Do not make it easy for someone to place something harmful in your drink. Do not allow others to bring you a drink. Go with them. Watch your drink the entire time. For the record, it does not matter if it is a guy or girl going to get the drinks.

If one is not allowed to leave an apartment by their own free will, this is false imprisonment in the mildest, kidnapping at its worst. Young ladies often fall victim to this on college campuses, as they do not perceive danger in most common situations and are far more trusting than they should be. While it may be hard, do not give in to coercion, doing so make it difficult to seek justice after the fact.

Sexual Grooming

Sexual grooming is by far the most devious and predatory form of sexual attack. Sexual grooming is where a predator lures his victim into a sexual relationship and keeps that relationship going using some form of reward and punishment. When thoroughly indoctrinated, the victim allows the assaults to continue because they perceive a benefit to its continuance. That benefit can easily be the lack of physical harm to themselves or their loved ones or the removal of some benefit they are receiving. While most often performed by adults on minors, grooming and coercion can be applied to anyone with low self-esteem, or in a dependent situation. Children often seek adult attention and approval, while parents particularly single or busy parents, tend to welcome additional help. Unfortunately, this situation can potentially allow predators an opportunity for sexual grooming. Let's break down how sexual grooming works:

Earning Trust – When it comes to winning the victim's trust, the best predators will often look exactly like a responsible caregiver. In fact, one will find many of these predators in positions that require trust like a pastor, coach, teacher, or counselor. While self-serving, the predator will often show genuine interest and concern for their victim. The unskilled predators will show an excessive level of attention to a particular individual over others.

Feeling Special – After earning the victim's trust, the predator will seek to make his victim feel special. This feeling of specialty is accomplished by filling a need specific to the victim or paying them excessive compliments or attention. Again, this is often the same behavior that a responsible caregiver will exhibit. The more unskilled predator will focus on one victim to the exclusion of others, but that is not always the rule.

Isolating the Victim – The predator will create situations where they will be alone with their victim. Predators can setup situations like babysitting, coaching, tutoring, or outings. This could be the first place where a predator deviates from the responsible caregiver, but again that is not always the case. Often the predator will try and work their way into a personal relationship with the victim and their family. Considered a "special friend," here is where predators will start asking their victim to keep secrets. They always begin with a test, then escalate until they know that they can trust their victim to keep quiet. My view is that short of a surprise birthday party or a

Christmas present; there should be no secrets between a child and an adult that is not their parent!

Desensitizing the Victim – At this stage, it should be obvious that one is dealing with a sexual predator. No caregiver will ever reach this point! The predator will begin to bring up sexual subjects, in the form of jokes or comments maybe even inappropriate pictures and videos. If done slowly and subtly enough, the victim does not feel shocked. The predator will escalate their actions to inappropriate touching or full nudity. Children are often curious about sex and may find this interaction pleasurable. Regardless, if the victim is a minor, this is a sexual assault, and the predator should be prosecuted for child molestation.

Sexual Contact – No matter how willing the victim, if they are under the age of consent this is statutory rape and a punishable sexual assault. Additionally, in many states, even if the victim is of legal age, if the predator is in a position of authority over the victim such as a pastor, teacher, coach or professor, any sexual interaction between the two is a criminal offense.

Rewards & Punishment – After the first sexual contact the predators will seek to maintain the relationship using their victim's emotional or material dependency on the predator. The victim often wishes to continue receiving whatever rewards the predator has set up. When rewards fail, the predator will use threats of blame, shame, or violence. After a few sexual encounters, the victim will start to deal with personal fears of humiliation if their secret ever comes out, and may continue the relationship out of fear, and self-shame. Parents and friends may notice a change in the victim's personality or behavior.

They may also see a different reaction from the victim particularly in the presence of the predator.

The deterrence of sexual grooming can be easy with checks and open communication. Teens should avoid being alone with any adult who is not a member of their immediate family. If one must be alone with a non-family member, limit the timespan and the number of occurrences. Young people should establish a pattern of check-ins with parents or friends. Notify someone when one's location changes or schedules change. One on one meetings should be in public places when possible. Ask questions about a person's intent. A true protector will not mind a parent or friend scrutinizing their actions when they are with their child. Most important young people should talk about any concerns they may have.

Countering Sexual Assaults

Only seven percent of all sexual assaults are stranger-on-stranger. This means there is often a level of familiarity between a victim and their assailant. How will one react if the attacker is a boss, teacher, close friend, boyfriend, or a family member? This type of attack is hard to prepare for as it violates a fundamental level of trust. If the possibility has never been imagined, then it is harder to see such attacks coming, and it is likely that one will fail to react in time. Victims of such trauma will often withdraw from family and friends, telling no one. They relive the experience every time they encounter their attacker.

A sex assault can begin in many ways. In many cases, there is no request for sex, and if there is any resistance by the victim, is brushed aside as an inconvenience. This is the time to think ahead and prepare.

I heard one young lady describe her assault as an out of body experience, feeling like she was not there. She was on the outside watching a friend abuse her. It took her years to come to terms with what happened to her merely because she had trusted this person so much and did not perceive the danger. Thus, remember even among trusted friends and family, the first two principles of self-protection are essential cornerstones.

If one has already been a victim of a sexual assault, part of deterrence is to tell someone to help prevent it from happening again. Quite often girls and women feel shame and believe it is somehow their fault. Often, victims think no one will believe them. I spoke with a young lady who believed that a boyfriend or husband could not rape a woman. She felt what had happened to her was no crime. Allow me to say this loudly. No means no, end of story. The inability to say yes is not consenting either. Regardless of what the perpetrator says, find someone you trust and tell them. A predator does not stop being a predator after the first victim, no more than a wolf quits being a wolf after it kills its first sheep. As a rule, if there is a first victim, there will be others. As a victim, there is pain, hurt, and humiliation, seek help with coping to ensure that this does not happen again or to anyone else ever.

The "Me Too Movement" has been one of the greatest things for young women who have been victims of sexual assaults. It shows that they are not alone, and even famous women have to deal with sexual assaults. It requires a degree of bravery to stand up to a predator and let them know that you are not willing to be a victim. It is a hard process, but people who feel that they can take advantage of others sexually, will hardly ever stop with only one victim. Larry Nassar, the USA Olympic gymnastics team doctor, assaulted over 260 girls ages 12 and up. Harvey Weinstein's alleged assaults were so prolific that the assaults became jokes in Hollywood films. Often times, people who have sexually assaulted someone without consequences will feel empowered and may become repeat offenders. So, it is important for victims to step up and say something.

The Random Predator

There are those in the world who receive pleasurable feelings of power from purposeless violence. Whom they hurt is not a concern, the very act of violence for violence sake is the motivation. These people tend to be very brutal in their actions. They often commit crimes with a partner or small entourage feeding on each other's excitement, which makes the crime even more horrific as each member pushes the other to go further.

The types of crimes that come to mind are crimes like the knockout game, the DC sniper shootings or the Ohio Highway sniper shootings, and people throwing bricks onto cars on the interstate. The actions one can take to deter this type of crime are minimal. The knock out game is only mitigated by being aware of one's surroundings and not allowing strangers into one's personal space. This type of crime is extremely difficult to defend against because it is an ambush style attack. The only applicable technique I can think of to counter this type of attack is the "**Defensive Fence**" drill. A technique outlined later in this book.

While all crimes can be placed into one of the major categories listed here, a person will not always have time to assess a predator's motives. To that end, one has to be diligent and observant taking action to deter any form of violence.

Chapter 3 – Practical Deterrence

From our earliest recollections, we can recall parents telling us do not talk to strangers, do not leave the yard, be careful, and if one has a very engaging parent, they will discuss good touches, bad touches and "If an adult tells you to keep a secret, you need to tell me immediately." In one paragraph I have outlined the extent of most parents' life lessons on deterrence. Much of what we learn we do by mimicking others. We get into the habit of locking the doors because that is what our parents did. We check the house at night because mom and dad did that growing up, virtually everything else a person picks up along the way.

The problem is, it is a brave new world and like it or not many parents of the young people I am trying to reach are clueless about the new challenges young people face. Yes, a thief is still a thief, and a bully is still a bully, but we are in the age of instant information. A bully does not go away the minute one makes it home safely. The magic of the internet means one's tormentors can attack them 24 hours a day. Additionally, those looking to feel powerful by putting others down receive instant gratification online with a certain sense of anonymity. General deterrence in the age of the smartphone requires that we kick things up a notch. We now need to be aware of our public and private profiles. Something most parents tend to know little to nothing about.

Common Sense

First, let us deal with the old-fashioned stuff. The bully that wants to be in one's face, and steal your lunch money is alive and well, as well as the guy who steals wallets. Thus, do not forget those lessons taught by your parents as they are still valid. So, we will make sure everyone has the basics. One of my favorite statements is "Common sense is anything but common." Many of the things that make basic deterrence effective are simple techniques, but they are not instinctive. We will list several of the simple deterrence techniques that should be practiced routinely. These are tried and true, but often ignored or dismissed.

When at Home

Lock the door – While that sounds simple almost 30% of burglars enter through an unlocked door or window.

Turn on the Alarm – If one has a home alarm turn it on when you and the family are in for the night. Just knowing that a blaring alarm will awaken the entire house and the neighbors will stop many home invasions.

Know your Neighbors – Knowing one's neighbors serves the purpose of knowing whom to trust and having an extra set of eyes should something happen. A friend next door will come looking when your alarm goes off in the middle of the day, which is a much quicker reaction than the response time of calling 911.

When Out and About

Lock your car – Beware of sliders, people who at the gas station slide into cars and steal items from the front seat. The easiest way to counter this is to lock the car doors immediately after exiting the vehicle.

Have your keys ready – Have your keys out and ready to open the car as you approach. Additionally, lock the doors immediately after entering.

Take your keys –Do not leave the keys in the ignition, not even for 10 seconds. Turn the car off and take the keys out. We have all seen the news where cars are jacked with kids in them because their parents did not turn the car off. I have channeled my inner psychic, and I clearly see that the world will not end if one takes the extra 10 seconds to pull the keys out of the ignition.

Take your keys anyway – Many cars now have keyless or keypad entry systems so people will lock their keys in the car intentionally. Get in the habit of taking your keys with you. This way thieves do not feel like they have hit the jackpot after breaking into the vehicle. Not only do they get items in the car, but they can take the vehicle as well.

Put it in the Trunk – Every Christmas we hear that people's cars were broken into and their packages were stolen. Well, newsflash, that does not just happen around Christmas. Predators do this all year round.

Put the Phone Up – We have seen people walk into poles while looking at their phone. What we do not see is the fact that holding a smartphone out advertises "Look what I have; come and steal it!" Additionally, it shows that a person is not paying attention to their surroundings or possible predators in the area.

Go as a Group – There is safety in numbers. While it is not a guarantee of safety, one is much safer in a group than alone.

When out Partying

Watch your drink – Roofies, also known as the date rape drug, are easy to get and are very effective. It does not take much to incapacitate a person, so do not leave a drink unattended. Other drugs like Fentanyl take only a few sprinkles to put a person out.

Do not get wasted – There have been many stories of people having had way too much to drink and woke up in someone else's bed. It is hard to claim sexual assault if a person is drunk enough to go willingly but too drunk to recall the details of what happened the previous night.

Go Home – If one is out and meets that hot guy or girl, do not be so anxious to go home with them. Do not let that one-night stand be the last stand. If they were truly hot in the club, it would not wear off overnight, unless one was looking at them through beer goggles. In that case, you will be glad you waited!

Again, some simple things to do to help deter would-be predators who are looking for a quick, easy target. This is by no means a complete list, but one would be amazed at how many crimes and violent acts could be prevented by following just these simple steps. Do not think "It will not happen to me." Set aside your ego, and take a few extra minutes to be safe.

Teens should Talk

The Teenage and young adult years are the strangest in our life. Everything is changing hormonally, socially, and physically. During this time, parents are just old, have no clue about anything, and like the Fresh Prince of Bel-Air said, "Parents just don't understand." I recall thinking that my dad was the dumbest man on the planet. It annoyed me that he was always there and always in my business! Sometimes I would just wish he would go away. However, by the time I graduated from college he became the smartest man on the planet. I wondered when did that happen.

Now that I am a parent, I want young people to know we get it. It is a teen thing. I have boys, and because I recall my teenage years, I laugh at them. When my youngest was playing basketball, I could tell him something he needed to add to his game or skill to improve on, and he would hear "**Whamp waa whaa Whamp**." However, the minute the coach or someone he admired said the same exact thing; it was like Lebron himself had descended from the clouds, sat down next to him and revealed the gospel of basketball to him. Kids, parent's get it. This is common, and even if your parents do not remember it, they were the same way when they were your age, even the smart ones! I think God has set it up so that your parents are the most annoying people on the planet.

I am banking on the fact that my teen and young adult readers will listen to me for just a few minutes because I am definitely not your parent! So here is the fact. If a person has caring parents, nothing enhances personal safety more than communicating with them.

A parent should always know your location and the company you keep. Additionally, if you decide to go elsewhere, a parent should know about your change in location. Yes, it takes an extra 20 seconds, but it helps with building trust.

This should be done every time simply to let potential predators know that someone knows where you are and with whom. It changes the risk versus reward equation.

With my boys, I would always tell them before your X, Y coordinates change I need to know about it. While they may think this is parents master plan to spoil the fun, I will tell the golden parental secret. We really do not care that much. What parents do care about is if something goes wrong where do we start looking? Who was there that saw what happened? We would also like the opportunity to question your choices. Quite often parents do not have a problem with what our children want to do just how they choose to do it. Some parents are uptight control freaks, but most are understanding when they know their child's objective.

This is a perfect time to use a personal experience as a teaching moment. A few years back, the day before Father's Day my youngest ignored the requirement to let his parents know where he was going. It was a quick five minutes from the house. He got into a car with a friend who had just gotten his driver's license the day before. My wife and I were out. We returned home, to find my oldest son in the driveway alone on the phone. He informed us that my youngest has been in a "minor" traffic accident. My wife insisted on retracing their route to try and find the site of the accident. When we got there, there was an ambulance on the scene. This was no minor accident. I asked the police officer about the tall kid with dreads. He told us he had been transported to the hospital. We found my baby boy in the emergency room with bleeding on the brain, a dislocated collarbone, a fractured number one rib, a lacerated liver, a lacerated kidney, and a deep cut on his face from his eye to his cheek. This singular moment of bad judgment and a failure to communicate led to four days in ICU and several months of recovery.

The purpose of communicating is not to destroy fun but to insert a more mature judgment into the decision-making process. The reason our son got into the vehicle with a friend was simply to get a half-price shake from Sonics, and his older brother did not want to take him. Had he followed our instructions, I probably would have told my oldest, a more experienced driver in a much safer vehicle, to take his brother to Sonics. By the way, it was probably about three months before he got that shake!

Technology Addictions

Technology is great. I know, I have spent my career creating, implementing, and customizing it. By itself, technology does not make life more or less safe. It is how we apply technology that enhances our security or increases our vulnerability. This security or vulnerability is amplified when combined with the power and reach of the internet. Unfortunately, with the introduction of each new toy, smartphone, game, or gear we use them all without a single consideration for our safety or the consequences of our actions. A simple moment of poor judgment combined with the internet can last for years and years to come. Social media has become the accepted norm for sharing information and exposing our vulnerabilities.

The World is Watching

Social media has been around since 1999 and online file sharing decades before that. These platforms (Facebook, Twitter, etc.) are meant for sharing information, ideas, pictures, and videos. In an online world, what you show and say will

NEVER go away! It will remain out there somewhere. Yes, one can delete the content from a given platform, but that only removes it from your personal account. It does not remove the content from others who may have viewed, saved or downloaded it.

While some young people think sexting is fun, be aware that you have no control over who sees or shares that information. If the subject is under 18, simply having such pictures can be criminal possession of child pornography, and sharing such is distributing child porn. This is true even if the pictures are selfies.

Contrary to popular opinion, having compromising pictures on your phone ONLY does not make them private or safe. A few years ago, 37 celebrities had their personal phone accounts hacked and their photos, mainly the nude photos, leaked on the internet. The ability to store pictures and information in some global cloud so that we can access it from our computers, phones or other devices exposes the potential for others to gain access to the same content. If one's nude photos are not for world viewing, then do not take nude pictures. In an online world, it is almost impossible to guarantee that they will not be hacked.

Social Media Safety

Being online allows up to the minute tracking of our friends and their activity. I see it all the time within my friend group on Facebook people often post their current location. So-and-so is checked in at this church, so-and-so is checked in at that gym, or so-and-so is at the airport leaving for vacation. The same happens on Snapchat, Twitter, Instagram, and even game consoles. I cringe every time I see this. Beware, not everyone that follows you is a friend, and the posts are not limited to just friends. Here are basic rules to follow:

- Do not post locations and times. This is an invitation for predators to come and rob your home.
- Post vacation pictures, only after returning home.
- Do not advertise valuables. Predators are watching.
- Do not be an online THOT! That is asking for trouble.
- Be mindful of what one says online. Do not say online what you would not say face-to-face.
- Remember you don't really know who you are talking to on a video game console. It is a predator's perfect hunting ground.

For the Guys

I love being able to help and mentor young men. I often tell mothers that they can raise a man, but no woman will be able to teach a man to be a man.

So, young men, I give you this. The greatest power is the ability to overcome one's self and not others as violence does not make a man. The hardest part of being a man is holding one's tongue and checking one's temper. Many times, people just want to have the last word and just cannot walk away. What is gained by this? It is hard to do the mature thing.

Keep your Hands to Yourself – Unless one is protecting themselves or another from immediate danger or harm, there is no valid reason to strike, punch, kick or in any other way assault another person. We are at a point in society where people are quick to draw a weapon. Unlike years ago a simple fist fight will not end many conflicts these days; the loser is now very likely to return with a weapon. What is your ego worth, surely not one's life? So, unless given no choice, keep your hands to yourself.

For the Ladies

Young ladies will notice that this book is targeted at keeping you safe. Many men find women easier to victimize, and young girls at times will put themselves in positions where they can be taken advantage of rather easily. There are other things that ladies should not do as it is asking for trouble.

Keep your Hands to Yourself – This is one of my biggest issues. I do not do double standards. I believe ladies are equal to men when it comes to rights. Women should be treated equally under the law, and in society as well. So, this logic should be simple. If men should not hit women, and women are treated as equal to men, then women should not hit men. Simple enough, right? Yet, many young ladies think it is okay to hit a man without them hitting back. That is a double standard that is just WRONG, WRONG, oh so WRONG!

I definitely do not believe in starting fights with anyone, and I have raised my boys never to start fights as well. Through some of the examples, it is easy to see that I have made my sons tolerate more than most before retaliating. One will also find that none of my guidelines for my sons make a distinction for one's gender be it male, female, or something in between. The simple line in the sand is if attacked, one has the right to fight back and do it decisively. Ladies, if you are going to start a fight, be prepared to get a fight. Do not assume one's sex or size provides special privileges. That is a double standard that may hold up in social settings but not in any court of law. Equal is equal, not only when it works in one's favor!

I share another story relative to my youngest son. During the boys' high school years, the family took a cruise to the Bahamas. A young lady was upset with my youngest. She decided to get in his face yelling, shoving, and pushing up against him. The first problem is no one has the right to make physical contact. My son pushed the girl away to insert defensive distance. It was aggressive and embarrassed the young lady. He could have been gentler about it, but one does not match aggression with equal force. One uses enough force to stop the violence and hopefully end the conflict. Common sense should have de-escalated this from the beginning. My son posed a bigger threat physically. He was not aggressive even after shoving her backward. By not advancing on her he demonstrated the desire not to engage further. She could have simply withdrawn, and the incident would have ended. The young lady instead was embarrassed and began slapping scratching and tearing at my son's clothes. My son said he did not mind the slaps as he blocked those, but she drew blood with her nails and tore one of his favorite shirts. At that time, he struck her. It was hard enough that after a single strike she went down and was unable to continue the fight.

After the ship's staff investigated the incident, the young ladies' parents were upset because my son hit a girl. The ships staff dismissed it because the footage showed her as the aggressor even though she was about a foot shorter than him.

The moral of the story ladies, keep your hands to yourself! One is never too cute or small to get hit back.

Methods for Mentors

Not every predator is an aggressor. Some of the most vicious predators are those that masquerade as victims. The current environment has empowered many women who have been sexually assaulted by men to step out of the shadows and seek justice. This is fantastic. But some girls and women have falsely accused men of sexual harassment, assaults, or even rape in an effort to seek revenge inflict harm or just get attention. This can be as devastating to a man as a physical assault.

Just the accusation can follow a person for years impacting every aspect of their life. The atmosphere on many college campuses is such that a student can be suspended or even expelled from school simply based on a mere accusation with no investigation, due process or anything even close. The stance of many is that "victims" deserved to be believed. This allows anyone to claim to be a victim, without questioning his or her motivations. As many of the victim's supporters will say "Why would they lie?" The why comes back to the risk versus reward calculation of all predators. With virtually zero consequences for making a false claim, particularly if the police are not involved, women can choose this tactic for any number of reasons.

In 2016 a Sacred Heart University student had consensual sex with two football players on a bathroom floor. After being exposed, she admitted that she made up the rape charges so that her promiscuity would not alienate a potential boyfriend. These two men are no longer in school. One lost his football scholarship over the lie. Additionally, in July of 2018, A woman in New York accused a man of rape because he would not give her a ride home.

I have personal experience with how a false accusation can change one's life. When I was about 24, I and several others who were enrolled in the same martial arts school would often workout on the playground with my heavy bag. Within months,

I got to know the neighborhood kids and a few of their parents. Some kids I would help with school projects, others wanted to learn a little bit about martial arts. Soon my apartment became the hangout for many of the teens and tweens. Some parents would even call asking if they could send their kids over for tutoring. On weekends, my roommate and I would often load up a bunch of the kids and take them out for a new experience like bowling, the arcade, or a different restaurant. I was amazed at the number of kids that had never had real Chinese or Italian food.

In those days, kids would just show up after school to do homework and hang out playing video games. That was fine with me as it kept some of the younger latchkey kids away from guys who would use the playground as a place to get drunk and occasionally harass them. Thinking back, I am not sure if their parents knew where their kids were half the time except on weekends when my roommate and I would take them out somewhere. My rule was "you could not go if your parents do not know."

That all changed when a 13-year-old girl, who lived upstairs told her friends I wanted to have sex with her. Her sister and another girl overheard her and called her out as a liar. Within five minutes, her sister and the friend were beating on my door to inform me as to what happened. I immediately went up to talk to her mother, to find the girl trying to minimize the damage telling her mother she was just kidding. Not my idea of a joke by any stretch of the imagination! Her mother said she had done this before to get attention.

I was relieved that this entire incident had been squashed within a half hour. That is when it hit me. I was extremely blessed this time. I had never been alone in my apartment with this little girl. I do not know if it was her mother's doing or not but anytime she showed up, at least one of her sisters were in tow. Then I quickly thought of all the other times I had been alone with any number of the other young ladies that lived in the neighborhood. What if one of them had accused me of touching them or some other inappropriate action. It was then that I changed how I interacted with all the kids in the neighborhood male or female. Here are some of the guidelines I set up to keep myself safe. They are effective for any coach, mentor or caregiver that wants to stay safe and avoid potential false accusations. I have added some additional guidelines for friends, as my son has been accused of sexual harassment by a former friend, after he slammed the door in her face, twice.

Avoid Being Alone

Avoid being alone with any young person that is not family with very rare exceptions. We can meet in the park, church or other public places, but not alone. If you must be alone with a young person for some reason like picking up a sick child for a friend or something of that nature, the parents are required to be informed the minute I arrived and minute that I dropped off their child. Make it a point to watch as the child informs their parents that they are home in the house and safe.

Always Include the Parents

Include parents in any communications one has with their child be it verbal or text messages. This keeps parents up to date on plans and intentions, and it serves as a backup as teens often forget, or wait until the last moment to inform parents. The teens that are part of my life will often ask me directly if I will do something for them. I first, make sure that the parent knows that they contacted me directly. This helps to reinforce the life lesson I wish to teach teens, let someone else know. If they talk to me directly, they will probably talk to some other adult directly. I know what my intentions are, I cannot say as much for any other adult. After that initial exchange, I include the parent in almost all other exchanges. If I am working with their teen on something like math homework, the parent knows that this is what we will be doing, and my exchanges are limited to just the homework. Any new discussions, I will include the parent once again.

Keep Parents Informed

Always let parents know where one is with their child. Whenever plans change, and I have someone else's child with me, I make it a point to keep the parents informed as to why the plan or location has changed, and the impact it will have. I include the child in the text just in case there is information they need to add. There may be reminders of special needs or medication that the parent may wish to convey. Additionally, if there is a significant other in your life, let that person know that your plans have changed as well.

Make it a Group Thing

Even among friends, make it a group thing. If there is a new member to the group of friends, make sure to educate that person about the rules regarding being alone. Even when just hanging around an apartment talking, make sure that one is not alone with new people. Quite often this will eliminate any miscommunications of intentions. It never hurts to be cautious when getting to know new people.

Be Consistent

Whatever practices one sets up be consistent with them. If one is consistent in actions and nature, any false accusations will show up as out of character. Parents will notice one's character and notice any change and warrant further investigation.

Face It Head-On

If one is ever falsely accused of anything, confront it immediately and without hostility. Yes, you will be angry but redirect that energy toward clearing your name. Address the allegation with someone in authority and present only the facts. This allows for prompt attention towards a quick resolution.

Chapter 4 – Preparation

The previous chapter outlines methods and actions to take to deter crime and violence, but there are some things that cannot be deterred. In those situations, we use the skills we have to respond as best we can at that moment. This is the purpose of training. Training ensures that we are prepared to recognize and act in a given situation both mentally and physically. When it comes to personal safety, one must always be able to think like a predator when entering a new environment and examine the location to answer the questions of who, what, when, where, how, and why. The order does not matter as long as one answers all these questions.

- **Who** will attack this location? Answering this question may also provide an answer to why.
- **What** is the target of the attack? Will this location be robbed or is this location more likely to be a subject of an attack on individuals like a school or a church?

- **Where** will an attack originate? Look around and see what the vulnerable points are. Take note of all the entrances, exits, hiding places.
- **When** will an attack happen? Ask if there are different times that a predator might choose to attack this location.
- **How** will someone attack this location? Is this location a place that someone will attack with a gun or knife, or is this a location vulnerable to a car bomb. This allows for focusing one's attention.
- **Why** will someone attack this location? Again the answer to this may also answer the who?

Answering all these questions in one's mind gives a place to start when observing the surroundings. Knowing a probable target of an attack, allows you to scout out the safest places to be.

Even after assessing one's environment and deciding that it has a low probability of being attacked, this does not mean that it has no probability of being attacked. Always keep in mind that every location could be a target. A perfect example of this is the 2018 Waffle House attack. In this attack, a shooter with an AR-15 walked in and started shooting people in the Waffle House for some unknown reason.

The gunman had no known reason to shoot-up the Waffle House. He was not a disgruntled employee and had no relationship with anyone in the Waffle House. This real-life example shows exactly how quickly an everyday activity can become a life-threatening event.

Being prepared with a plan gives one a head start in being safe anywhere. Think about the "What ifs" in life. One should examine their life and seriously consider some real life "what if" scenarios and think about how to handle them. The situations listed below are generic but serve as a great starting point.

Things to Think About

If this book is part of a family safety discussion, here are a few things to keep in mind. The proper way to deal with some issues varies based on the age of the victim, so each person should discuss their approach to solving the problem. An open discussion gives insight into how children or teens approach problems. Adults should add their wisdom by offering better ways to handle some situations. Here is a list of scenarios to have a safety discussion about. I would even suggest having these types of discussions at church youth and young adult meetings as well as scout meetings. Even among peer groups take the time to bring up practical discussions, Safety should be a concern of everyone.

Bullying Scenarios – What will I do if?
- What to do if physically threatened in the neighborhood, work or at school by a bully?
- What to do if a bully is physically aggressive?
- What to do if pushed by one's partner?
- What to do if punched or struck by one's partner?

Home Invasions – What will I do?
- What does one do if one enters their home to find that it has been robbed?
- What if one walks in, and there is someone there?
- What if someone breaks in while one is at home, i.e., a home invasion?

- What if the home invader is armed?

Public Areas – What will I do if?

- What if some stranger approaches while one is alone?
- What if an armed stranger approach while one is alone?
- What if one is asked by a stranger to approach their car?
- What if some stranger points a weapon from a vehicle?
- What if a family friend asks one to get in the vehicle unexpectedly?
- What if one is asked to go somewhere with a family friend?

Sexual Advances – What will I do if?

- How does one deal with unwanted sexual advances from a male or female?
- What would one do if someone is groping one's body parts, but, not using force?
- What would one do if someone is groping one's body parts and using violence to force compliance?
- What would one do if they were using their physical strength violently?

Rethink the above sexual assault scenarios. This time, go through each with a particular type of predator in mind. How would one handle the situation if the predator is a stranger, a teacher or employer, friend, a boyfriend, and finally a family member? How much resistance is one willing to use in each case? There are a lot of options and actions between, "I will let it happen," and "I will do whatever it takes to stop them." The chances are high that you, the reader, will face one of the scenarios outlined here. Lifelong trauma happens when ill-equipped to handle a situation. Considering the possibility is the first step to being able to deter an assault and deal with the predator.

Think of different scenarios that could quickly escalate to violence and think of how one would handle them. The more one practices this thought pattern, the easier it is for one to recognize potentially dangerous situations in everyday life, and begin to improve one's techniques of detection, and deterrence.

Special Circumstances

Of all the types of what-if scenarios to think about, there are two that I would like to draw special attention to and that is the home invasion and active events. An active event is defined as any event taking place in which a predator is actively seeking to cause injury or death to as many people as possible. Most of us see this in the active shooter events, but active events can unfold with guns, knives, bombs, or vehicles. If one concentrates on only one type of active event, they leave themselves open to all the others.

I pick these two situations simply because they are very impersonal and evolve so quickly that standard methods of deterrence tend to fall short in keeping one safe. These situations require preparation.

Home Invasions

The idea of a home invasion is immensely scary. A home invasion may start accidentally as a burglary where the predators just happen to enter while someone is present or it could be the predator's intention to catch his or her victims at home. Regardless, if there is any place on earth one should feel safe it is at home. But that is where all the good stuff thieves want to steal is kept. Additionally, people do not carry cash anymore. So, predators find it more profitable to do home invasions and get debit card numbers while taking valuables as well. Whatever the motive, being home when a stranger enters is never a good thing. It is not something one wishes to experience as a victim, and it is usually not something the predator wants either, but they often come prepared to deal with just such a situation.

Therein lies the problem, predators come ready to deal with the fact that someone may be home. But regular people assume they are safe at home. When someone kicks open the front door is the wrong time to consider personal safety. If one has not planned for such a situation beforehand, during an actual home invasion is a little too late.

Families should have emergency plans for events like fire or home invasions. Most home break-ins occur between 6:00 am and 6:00 pm. This is also the time when teens are most likely home alone. The most dangerous break-ins occur late at night when the predator expects someone to be home and is looking for someone to victimize. In any case, one should plan for the various scenarios.

For the teen that comes home and is there alone before parents arrive, there should be a plan to ensure one's safety before entering the home and while home alone. This is also true for any young adults that live alone. How does one deal with someone breaking in? Are there alternate ways out of the home or apartment?

The next plan is for families. What does one do when someone breaks-in during waking hours and the family is home? What does one do if someone breaks in while the family is sleep? These should be plans that every family has. If there is a plan for a fire, there should be a plan for a home invasion.

Many of the tactics listed in the next section on "Active Events" will apply in a home invasion. Additionally, the "**Home Invasion**" drill found later in this book explains how to test different home invasion scenarios safely.

As a special note to teens living at home, parents will gladly give their life to save yours. Many parents will avoid firing a gun if there is a possibility that their children will be in the line of fire. Once a plan for dealing with a home invasion has been established do your best to follow the plan! Personally, I will react much more decisively knowing my children are out of the house and safe.

Given the possible scenarios of a home invasion look at the two locations in your home in which most of your time is spent. One of those locations should be the bedroom. Now plan how to escape if someone enters the front, or back or side door. Is there a way to escape the house? Many will find that they live in homes or apartments that leaves them trapped. The windows may be too high off the ground or impossible to open quickly. This is where one must plan to survive up to 20 minutes alone.

The average response time to a 911 call is about 10 minutes. If one is able to escape a home invasion, do so and call the police from the neighbor's house. If escape is not possible then plan how to survive until the police arrive. Plan a way to barricade oneself into a safe area that will hold up until help arrives. The second option is to have an effective method to fight back in many cases this may be a firearm.

In many home invasion discussions and training sessions, I have encountered families where the possession of firearms is a nonstarter. The idea of a teen having access to a firearm is unacceptable to them. Additionally, some families are not allowed to have firearms in the home. I completely understand this. Whatever the reason, my suggestion to these families is a nonlethal solution such as pepper ball guns or pepper spray. Such chemical deterrents can allow an opportunity to effectively fight back and escape, especially if combined with an aluminum tee-ball bat. The pepper ball gun provides an effective way of incapacitating a predator from a distance while the bat can easily disable them. As this is a nonlethal assault, one must be more aggressive in attacking the predator knowing that the goal is not to drive off the predator but to escape the home. Seeing that a victim is willing to fight back may make the predators more violent once they have successfully entered the home. But at the same time, the pepper gas or spray will serve to buy time.

As a family, this is a point in the book for discussion and planning. What will you do if? My opinion is that blind compliance with a predator's demands is not a strategy for survival. I would prefer it if my family's survival is based on a plan of action and not the charity of predators.

The Active Event

We see it often on the news the carnage caused by active shooters in our schools, malls, workplaces, and nightclubs, as people run for their lives trying to get away. Everyone is vulnerable to active events. The predator's motivations will fit into the categories listed previously, but their interaction is not related to the individual victims directly. One must always be aware and prepared for such events. While the likely hood of any individual reading this book being involved in an active event is low, there is always the possibility.

The most common locations for active events are schools, including colleges, and workplaces. While many with agendas will argue about guns and gun control, understand that individuals who are intent on causing mass injuries will find a way. We have seen mass attacks with machetes and vehicles, and even bombs made out of pressure cookers. The problem is not the tool but the individuals whose intent it is to hurt people.

As guns are often the weapon of choice, understand that in the United States, there are about 300 million guns in the hands of U.S. citizens. One can assume that the next shooter already has their weapon, and little can be done to stop their attempt at this time. The best we can hope for is preventing or minimizing the damage they cause. The idea of "See Something Say Something" is the best thing to do in order to control and prevent this type of tragedy. Forget the idea of being looked at as a snitch; the life one saves maybe one's own. However, like in the case of the Marjory Stoneman Douglas High School shooting, "See Something Say Something" failed miserably at the local, state, and federal levels. So, one must be prepared to act on one's own behalf.

I cannot state it enough, that with knowledge comes responsibility. If one is old enough to read and comprehend this book, then it is your responsibility to protect your own life. By reading this, you are more knowledgeable than most and have the responsibility to act if ever involved in an active event. Additionally, one had the responsibility to tell if they know of an event that is planned. We think the teachers and staff are supposed to protect students, but they cannot protect students from what they do not know, and other students often know about a threat long before teachers do. The best way to survive an active event is to prevent it from happening to start with. If you know something, say something.

While I do not believe in living a life of fear, I do not believe in living unprepared either. There is no way to predict when and where an active event will happen. So, any time one is in a new location or environment perform the "**I'm Billy Bad**" drill. Use this to begin working out a plan. Even if one cannot come up with all the answers, the start of a plan is better than no plan at all.

Depending on who asks, there are several methods of dealing with active events. Homeland Security uses "Run, Hide, Fight." Others use the ALICE method, which is Alert, Lockdown, Inform, Counter, Evaluate. While any method is better than none at all, I like the method the FBI came out with long ago. It is the **ABC** method. The **A** is for **Avoid and Alert**, **B** is for **Barricade/Block the Door**, and **C** is for **Conceal or Confront**.

Avoid and Alert

At the first sign of trouble **AVOID** the immediate threat and **ALERT** others to the potential danger. Under no circumstances does one want to stick around and see what happens. You can watch it on the news. After alerting others to the threat, take every measure possible to avoid the predator or predators. In this case, distance is one's friend. Put as much distance between yourself and the threat as possible. While leaving the area, use cover and concealment as protection. At any time during an active event if the opportunity presents itself to escape, take it!

On the way out you may come across wounded individuals. If they are unable to move on their own, leave them behind. Yes, that sounds cold and heartless, but without medical training moving a wounded person may do more damage than good, and the last thing that rescuers need is to add yet another body, namely yours, to the death toll.

On the way out of the area, tell others not to enter. If one encounters authorities, put your hands up and follow their instructions. Do not run toward or grab onto police as they enter the building. They do not know who the shooter is and those actions can cause the police to mistake you for the predator. Law enforcement's first goal is to neutralize the threat. Their secondary goal is to help the victims in the aftermath.

Barricade – Block the Door

As an active event unfolds if one is unable to escape the area, the best option is to barricade oneself in a room and remain as quiet as possible by turning out the lights and turning off the cell phone ringers. Remember many schools and college campuses send text messages to warn of danger. Do not allow that notification to be what gives one's location away. Understand that locking the door often will not be adequate. If there is a window that a predator can break and reach an arm through to unlock the door, then the lock is useless. Barricading a room can be a little tricky but is not impossible. It requires a bit of creativity and possibly some fast thinking. A couple of simple methods are listed here for barricading doors if needed.

Generic Barricade

When choosing to barricade a door, one may need to address any windows located in the door. Cover the windows if they provide a clear view of the room to prevent the opportunity for the shooter to target people like fish in a barrel.

The simplest barricade is a wall of objects. Stack as many objects in front of the door as possible, This should include tables, chairs, desks, or even trash cans. The more items a person would have to go through to gain access to the protected space the better. While this is best for doors that open in, it can also be used for doors that open out. The heavier the objects that can be placed against the door the better.

Doors Opening Inward

Screwdriver / Wedge – A screwdriver or an open textbook can be used as a wedge to prevent the door from opening.

Chair Under Door Knob – A high backed chair can be wedged under a doorknob using friction to prevent the door from opening.

Flat on the floor – Lying flat on the floor with one's feet at the door will work to stop a door from opening. While this method may still result in injury or death, the predator still must move one's physical body out of the way before they can enter the room. It could effectively protect others in the room.

Doors Opening Outward

A Belt on Hinge Arm – a belt around the hinge arm of a door will prevent the door from opening.

Zip Ties – Zip ties on hinge arms or doorknobs can be used to prevent entry.

Barring the Door – Using the door handle several items can be used to prevent entry into a room. A screwdriver, broomstick, folding chair all can be used in order to avoid entry into a room.

After barricading the door, move away. An active shooter will often shoot through a door in frustration if unable to gain entry to the room or if it appears that someone is holding the door closed.

Conceal – If Practical

Stationary Concealment means that we are reaching the bottom of the barrel of options. I dislike concealment simply because most hiding places, like closets, under beds, or under desks are small compartments that leave one trapped and unable to fight back. If one has no intention of fighting back, then do what it takes to find the best hiding place. If possible bring something to use as a weapon just in case. However, at this point, if one is unable to avoid or barricade a door, concealment is the best bad option left.

Confrontation – Fight to Live

Understand that there is no negotiating with an active shooter once the shooting has started. The shooter's sole intent is to kill. With that understanding, I cannot stress this enough. If one does nothing, one will die. If one chooses to fight back, one might die. However, the math is simple; a 50% chance at life is better than a 100% chance of death. As a group, there is the ability to distract and swarm a predator, he may kill some, but he cannot kill everyone. Thinking, I will let someone else do it, is the prey mindset and a death sentence for all. There are no other options that one can control. This is a hard thing for a college student to consider, and even harder for a high school, or middle schooler, but this is the world we live in so let's deal with the idea of a life and death situation head-on.

Now that the decision has been made to confront the predator commit wholeheartedly to the fight with extreme violence of action. Evaluate the immediate surroundings and consider what is available as a weapon. Chairs, brooms, books or even cell phones are viable weapons. After choosing a method of attack, find a strategic position. Standing in front of an active shooter is never a good idea. Attacking from the side or behind offers many advantages especially if the predator has a rifle. If in an area with multiple people, look to coordinate everyone's efforts. Some will panic and freeze, others are willing to act, but have no idea what actions to take. If there is no leader to rally them to attack, people will typically run in no particular direction. It is the natural reaction of a group to follow a strong leader. Just knowing the information in this book makes you a qualified leader. Understand that failure to act will most likely result in the injury or death of one's self and others.

When confronting a predator, one must neutralize the threat. Taking a weapon from the predator is not neutralizing the threat. One never knows if there is an additional weapon be it a handgun, knife or something else that may be used as a weapon. Neutralizing the threat means making sure the predator is unable to continue their assault. If the predator is taken to the ground, the first time they attempt to get up the fight is not over. Find a way to render them immobile. Shoelaces, a shirt, curtains anything that can be used to restrain the predator will work. If required a kick to the head or any other method to render them unconscious will work. An active shooter has demonstrated a willingness and capacity to kill, so any resistance they provide is a continued threat.

Chapter 5 – Seeking Help

In modern society, we have grown to expect that if there is a problem, we call 911 and all will be well. It is not until we are the victim of a crime of violence that we realize how helpless we have allowed ourselves to become. We have given ourselves over to the idea that we are not responsible for our own safety because the police will take care of us. This is a delusional idea given the events we see daily on the nightly news. We prepare our homes for fire with smoke detectors and fire extinguishers and even have fire plans. However far less of us prepare for a home break-in, even fewer are prepared to deal with a home invasion give the fact that about 65% of all break-ins occur while someone is at home. We do not expect to be robbed walking down the street. We do not expect to be attacked and raped while jogging in the park. These are not things that happen in polite society. However, the reality is we do not live in "polite" society.

The human animal is a violent creature, and unless one has the funds to hire an entourage of bodyguards, it is impossible to outsource our protection. Even our minors need to understand the importance of protecting themselves. In short, you are your own first, best, and the last line of defense.

There will be times when one cannot go it alone. What do you do when you need to seek help? For an obvious crime in progress, call the police, but not everything is a crime, and often, the idea of going to the police is not something people are comfortable with. There is no emotional support when calling the police so for many young people this is not a comfortable first step. So, what does one do?

Where to get Help

Of all the sections in this book, I have found this one section to be the hardest to write. I now understand the distress that many teens have with wanting help but not knowing where to go to get it. There is no national 911 type number for general help, and the police have very limited power where they cannot prove a crime has been committed. So, in this section, I would like to try and put together a set of resources that will help when the police cannot. I had to consult an outside resource who was a principal for years and is now a college professor. Much to my surprise, the best answer was easier than I thought.

For those readers who are still in school, any school, the first and realistically the most important place to go for help is one's school guidance counselor! Yes, the same person that helps decide what classes to take, and put together college transcripts is a trained professional counselor. They have the know-how and the contacts to get the help one needs. Better still, they are obligated by law to keep personal discussions confidential. Many teens do not seek help because of feelings of embarrassment or fear of reprisals. A guidance counselor can help and offer support when needed.

One problem is that many students do not have a close, trusting relationship with a guidance counselor. The guidance counselor is usually perceived to be someone you talk to about classes. If this is the case, almost every student has one teacher, past or present, that they have connected with. Go to that teacher. They will help you find help, can be there when going to the guidance counselor. They too are required by law to keep that conversation confidential. In short, the first place to go for help is within the school.

Teens or young adults can also get help from that one friend or that one mentor who will speak life into them and be there no matter what. Not everyone has a person like this, but if one does, that is always a good place to get help. I tell parents every child should have a person that they can trust and talk to that will give them good counsel when they either do not want to or need help going to a parent. For those who do not have a deep support structure, let me offer some other resources.

People & Places for Help

If one feels they need help and school is not a place one can turn. Here are some contacts that may prove helpful.

National Safe Place Network – This is a national network of organizers that are trained to provide immediate aid and relief to teens and young people in crisis 24 hours a day.

Rape, Abuse & Incest National Network – 1-800-656-4673 This is a 24-hour hotline that can place one in contact with resources that can help any survivors of rape, abuse or incest.

National Suicide Prevention Lifeline – 1-800-273-8255 If one is feeling suicidal, please access this resource. Nothing is worth your life.

Interacting with the Police

Often the first thing people think of when trouble erupts is to call 911. While this is not a bad thing, there needs to be a single question one must ask before calling 911. Am I safe for now or am I as safe as I can be? Only when one is safe to do so call 911. If one is in imminent danger stopping to call 911 may not be the best option. If a person is breaking into one's home, and the options available are call 911, get a weapon or escape to the neighbors, the first choice should be to escape to the neighbors followed by securing a weapon and finally calling 911. There will be a delay between the time one calls 911 and the time help arrives. Do what it takes to ensure one is alive and well when help arrives. In most cases that will be about 10 minutes, but at times it can be much longer.

As a Victim

After contacting the police, be prepared to share all available information. Keep any speculation or conjecture out of one's discussion. The officer who arrives on the scene will already have an information deficit do not fill the void with information that may not be true. It is important that officers work from the most accurate information available. Personal speculation muddies that already limited pool of knowledge. Be prepared to give an address and location, the reason for the call, and exactly what is needed. Most importantly do not ramble.

Be prepared to answer questions. The call taker is trying to capture as much information as possible. Answer with what you know, do not speculate. If the call taker asks, "Do you know what they looked like?" Answer clearly yes or no. If one did not get a good look at the perpetrator, do not try to help by guessing. If one tells the dispatcher, "It was a large heavy-set male, about six-foot-tall, wearing a black cap, and flannel jacket" this is good information. If one goes on to add "He sounded white." That is an assumption, not information. But, if one adds he spoke with what sounded like a heavy British accent. That is information. Do not hang up on the call taker as they will continue to try and ask for additional information. If one has to, simply put the phone on speaker or put the phone down.

When Cops Arrive

When police arrive, let them take control of the situation as per their training. They will ask questions, many of them, you will have already answered when you first called 911. Do not get frustrated remain calm and answer the question. Quite often the call taker does not relay every piece of information to the first officer on the scene. Allow them to lead the conversation. Be prepared to tell them exactly why you called 911 and what happened. Quite often there is not an arrest. They may make someone leave the premise, or have a discussion with them as an alternative.

Dealing with Officers

Let's talk about police and personal safety; this is about as good a time as any to discuss how to interact with law enforcement. For better or worse, police are a cross-section of society. They embody the good, the bad, the ugly, and the downright criminal. Like the general public, the majority of law enforcement officers are great individuals. The problem is one bad cop can ruin the reputation of an entire department, and many times social media magnifies that narrative with a disproportionate number of videos and views of officers behaving badly. In general, law enforcement officers are great people. Most truly want to serve and protect.

When contacting the police in an emergency or out in public be respectful, courteous and honest. Allow the police officer to help. Many people have a problem with law-enforcements take over tactics when they arrive on the scene. Understand this is their training. For their safety and yours, they are required to control the environment because threats may come from anywhere. In many cases, they are preventing or preparing for threats that the average person would never think about.

Even when you have a problem with a particular officer, there are systems in place to handle that. The mist of a crisis or on the side of the road is not the place for it. Get their name or badge number and deal with the issue at a later date.

Chapter 6 – Tactics for a Fight

When no other form of de-escalation has worked, a fight is inevitable. The most valuable skill in any fight is the ability to assess a predator's strengths and weaknesses. As everyone is different, every fight will be different as well. The faster this assessment and adjustment is made to the predator the more likely one is to be victorious. Great fighting techniques are useless if the tactics are flawed. We must understand how to use what we know, and what the predator reveals to us to the best of our ability.

Use Your Fear

Fear is a part of every fight, and while many may not see it as a tool, if controlled, it can be used as an extra weapon or a superpower. An understanding of fear can be used tactically to determine the best techniques to use. Coping with fear is a critical factor in self-defense. A person is expected to be afraid but must avoid panic.

When a person is afraid, the body dumps adrenaline into the blood. The blood vessels in the extremities constrict, and blood concentrates in the large muscles, body core, and the brain. Things seem to move in slow motion because the brain is working at an accelerated rate assessing the best reactions to the situation at hand. The mind will pull from the techniques and tactics that it has memorized. We call this muscle memory. Internally, the brain has created shortcuts that allow for quick execution of trained responses. During this time, many of the pain receptors shut down. Fine motor skills no longer work, but large muscle movements are enhanced, and one's awareness of the threat is heightened. Often one's strength is increased and reaction times shortened. Knowing that this is going to happen, ensure that your techniques include, powerful movements such as knees, elbows, and kicks.

Panic is the extreme end of fear, which is the worst possible reaction. When panicked, the brain shuts down all reasonable thoughts and responses. Often the panic-stricken person is so frozen with fear that even running is not an option. To avoid panic one must control fear through training and preparation. Training will not eliminate fear, but it will prevent fear from escalating to the point of panic. This is the reason soldiers train repeatedly. The first few times one does something it is a learning process both mentally and physically. After continued training, these actions begin to become repetitive and the mind starts to build shortcuts or muscle memory. When acting under duress and fear, the mind does not think of new techniques and strategies it adapts and applies what it already knows. The fastest techniques are those that have been conditioned so much that the body reacts so quickly that it was never a conscious thought.

Strike First

The average street fight lasts nine seconds. Thus, striking first is important. Throwing the first punch is not as important as landing the first blow. The one who lands the first effective strike will often win the fight. Using defensive techniques like the **"Defensive Fence"** help to ensure that one does not succumb to a sudden attack and is prepared to counter. Every offensive technique a predator uses creates an opportunity for a counterattack. When a conflict becomes physical, I suggest responding with overwhelming force. There is no benefit to an evenly matched fight. Whenever possible, use any opportunity or advantage to win the fight. Often landing that first strike can easily be that advantage.

Strike Fast

Attack fast! Smaller individuals should train to strike with as much speed as possible. We all know that a big man can hit hard, but a small person can overcome the lack of size with speed. I can push a person slowly with a telephone pole, and it will not hurt, but if I hit them with a baseball bat swung as quickly as possible it would definitely cause pain and suffering. The same holds true when striking quickly with a small surface area, such as the knuckles, knees or elbows. A quick strike to a soft part of the body can go a long way in ending a fight.

Strike Frequently

Never assume that one blow will finish a predator. While it may, this is a poor assumption to make, and a delay between strikes may allow recovery and a counterattack. Strike frequently selecting multiple areas of the head, body and even the lower legs. If a predator has no idea where the next blow will land, he or she is more likely to retreat or curl up into a protective ball. Look at the vulnerabilities chart later in this chapter and choose multiple areas to target in a counterstrike combination and train to strike these areas.

Strike Furiously

In addition to striking fast and frequently, a person should strike with the ferocity of a wild animal. The objective is to protect oneself by disabling the predator. A street fight is not a ten round boxing match. Try to end a fight in 30 seconds or less. Use the hips to twist and strike with power and purpose. Every technique that is thrown should be intended to cause bodily harm. Train to strike six inches into the target. If a strike ends at the tip of the predator's nose, it does not matter how fast or frequently one punches. It will have no effect. A strike should end deep within the target transferring all its energy to the predator. Striking deep is what causes pain, and bodily harm. Such strikes will hopefully end the fight.

Move Forward

Begin the attack moving forward as forward momentum helps generate power. It is almost impossible to create enough power to cause significant damage while moving backward. If driven back by the predator, step to the side out of the line of attack giving a brief moment to counterattack as the predator has to adjust to one's new location. Strike with counter techniques that can force the predator into a defensive posture.

Target the Face

The head and neck area have more vulnerable areas than any other part of the human body. Look to target the throat, eyes, nose, ears, and even the collarbone. They are excellent targets that are easily damaged or broken. However, do not get so fixated on attacking just the face that other targets are ignored. A good punch to the solar plexus will often bring the predator's head low to be finished with a knee. Additionally, a knee to the pubis can easily cause the hip bones to separate making standing or walking painfully difficult.

Disrupt Their Plan

Mike Tyson once said, "Everyone has a plan until they get punched in the mouth." A first tactic should be to disrupt the predator's plan. Landing that first blow may end the fight, but it must be something decisive. If one's stature does not allow for the generation of great power, then concentrate on combinations that will allow one to attack multiple vulnerabilities.

This is an important concept to remember when doing the **"Abduction"** or **"Bully Beat Down"** drills and their variants. Whatever the predator's plan is, choose techniques that will make them think of protecting themselves first.

Fair is Foolish

If you have done everything to avoid a fight, and cannot, then do everything needed to win. If one finds it necessary to fight, understand there is no limit on what is fair. Sticks, stones, chairs, and tables are viable weapons. In a fight, the predator does not present their resume to show how good a fighter they are and there is no way of knowing if the predator is a grandmaster or a thug that has never thrown a punch. Assume that every predator is Bruce Lee, Jackie Chan, Chuck Norris, and Mike Tyson all rolled up in one. If given any chance to disable the predator and end a fight do not pass it up. In the end, the fairest fight is the one you win! This may not be appropriate for the schoolyard fight, but if facing serious bodily harm, hit them with a chair and run!

Dealing with Size

The size of a predator is a definite factor in how one should determine a fight strategy. When facing a larger predator, there are some general rules which should be considered. They are as follows:

Fight Inside – The shorter person should fight inside the range of the taller person to neutralize their reach advantage. Striking with knees and elbows can equalize the power advantage as well.

Strike Low – The range of a puncher can be neutralized with oblique kicks on the outside of the knee. Even if the strike is not effective the technique will cause the predator to reconsider their strategy giving time for your counterattack.

Use Angles – Seeking effective angles of attack can go a long way to neutralizing a predator's size advantage. Remain outside of a predator's zone of power unless one can take the predator's center.

Fight in 3D

Many people, particularly the untrained, think only of punching to the head when fighting. While this makes it important to protect the head, it shows a fatal flaw in many predators' attacks. They ignore the body, legs, and knees. Leaving them open to body shots and low kicks. When developing combinations, attack the entire body. While the headshot will often end the fight immediately, a punch to the stomach will often bring the hands low to allow a clean punch to the head. Additionally, an oblique kick to the outside of the knee or a foot sweep can hamper a predator's ability to stand and often break their will to fight.

Break the Line of Attack

In a street fight, most attacks are a linear barrage of punches. By slipping to the side out of the way, one breaks the line of the attack. This forces the predator to either attack off-balanced or to reposition himself to start a new attack. This break in the predator's rhythm allows for a quick counterattack. A quick pivot on the lead foot or a quick step forward at a 45-degree angle will allow one to move out of the line of attack while remaining close enough to counter.

Attack from the Rear

In addition to breaking the line of attack. One should seek to get behind the predator. Getting behind a predator is my favorite move as it neutralizes a person's most powerful weapons. It is hard for a predator to punch or kick a person who is striking from the rear. While it is not sporting, I did say fair is for fools. This allows for a rear naked or bar-arm choke.

Use the Ground

Many do not understand the benefit of a throw or takedown. In an urban environment, concrete or asphalt is unyielding. No matter how hard one can punch or kick, the ground hits harder. Using trips and throws can have a devastating impact on the entire body especially the head. Takedowns, throws, and sweeps are fantastic techniques to quickly stun or incapacitate a predator long enough to get away. Additionally, it is important to learn how to fall to minimize impact just in case you are the one being taken to the ground.

Pick Your Targets

Just striking a predator will not guarantee victory. In most cases, the majority of the body surfaces where a strike may land has no strategic value at all. In a real fight, one will not get to land many strikes. Remember most fights last a total of nine seconds. Thus, it is important that every strike landed be purposeful and well-aimed. The human body gives us a few key spots that we may attack effectively. Striking these areas can cause either extreme pain, debilitating injury or mortal wounds. The following diagram is a list of vulnerable areas to target.

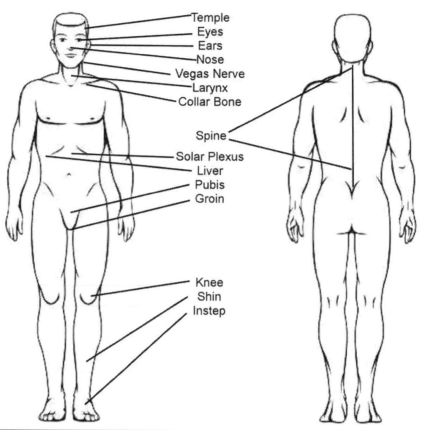

Temple
Eyes
Ears
Nose
Vegas Nerve
Larynx
Collar Bone

Spine
Solar Plexus
Liver
Pubis
Groin

Knee
Shin
Instep

Target	Technique
Chin	palm strike, hook or round punch, uppercut, elbow, headbutt
Collarbone	Hammer fist, knife strike, downward elbow, ax kick
Ears	Palm strike, grab
Eyes	Punch, fishhook, eye stab, elbow, headbutt
Groin	Front knee, front kick, palm strike, heel kick
Kidney	Hook or Round punch, round kick
Knee	Oblique kick, round kick, side kick
Larynx	Knife hand, fishhook, front punch

Liver	Hook punch, heel kicks, round kick, front punch, side kick.
Nose	Hammer fist, front punch, palm strike, elbow strike, headbutt
Pubis	Palm strike, round knee, front knee, front kick
Solar plexus	Uppercut, round knee, heel kick, front kick.
Spine	Reverse elbow, downward reverse elbow
Temple	Elbow, reverse elbow, round punch, headbutt

Additionally, there are areas of the body to avoid such as the arms, back, chest, and upper thigh. While the strikes may cause some pain, it will require repeated strikes to disable a predator. In fact, the femur is as dense as concrete. The chances of doing severe damage while kicking to the femur are minimal.

An area of question is the shin. One never knows who has training and who does not. In many cases kicking a person in the shin hurts them significantly. However, people who train in Muay Thai and soccer players tend to have very tough shins. If a first strike has no effect, then eliminate the shin as a target.

Practice Combinations

When building combinations start by keeping them simple and easy so that they can be used quickly and effectively. Never use more than about four moves in a single combination, but be able to move from one combination to another seamlessly. The intent is to quickly reset one's footing or body position between combinations if needed.

Here I have listed several classic combinations used in boxing and kickboxing. Start by training in a mirror to first see what right looks like. Do this enough times until you can close your eyes and know what right feels like. Settle on about 15 offensive and 15 defensive combinations to be the mainstay of your fighting techniques.

Note: Each style has its own names for very similar techniques, I have labeled these techniques using boxing and kickboxing terms. Whatever name you choose to give these techniques, make them your own. Make them fit within the style of fighting you are comfortable with.

Offensive Combinations

Offensive combinations should play to one's strengths. I am not the fastest, but I am good at concealing my true intent. For me, my offensive combinations have at least three techniques simply because I assume that the first technique is not going to land. Additionally, as mentioned earlier I use these techniques moving forward with a quick step or push step to close the distance.

1. Jab, Cross, overhand left
2. Jab, Jab, Hook
3. Jab, Cross, Hook.
4. Jab, cross, uppercut, hook
5. Jab, hook, hook
6. Jab, Uppercut, hook
7. Backfist, cross, rear low round kick
8. Sidekick, backfist, cross
9. Front kick, jab, cross

Defensive Combinations

Defensive combinations start with a block, slip, or some other evasive move. This puts one out of the optimal position to strike a predator, but it lets one take advantage of any opening that an attack will leave. The following are a few of my personal favorite defensive strikes.

1. Outside block, low heel kick
2. Outside block, cross, hook
3. Outside block, elbow, knee
4. Inside block, knife strike, low hook
5. Inside block, cross, round kick or knee
6. Double arm block, round knee, front or reverse elbow
7. Low block, low round kick.
8. Low block uppercut, round
9. Slide back repeatedly, heel kick, Cross, elbow

Build Your Own Combos

I have given just a few combinations. There is an almost endless list of techniques that can be used in series. Try different combinations while training. Make it a conscious effort to write down combos that work. Watch others while training and borrow the combinations they use that work for you. Do not be afraid to discard techniques that do not work. Often techniques that work for friends are not quite right for you. Change them or discard them. This is the purpose of training to use all your techniques and a variety of combinations. Put together a personal list and practice those routines repeatedly. One wants to build that muscle memory to be able to call upon techniques without thinking about it. For those of you who are not martial artists, limit combinations to three moves. Make sure they can be executed quickly. Make sure one can strike on multiple levels and from multiple directions.

Chapter 7 – Drills & Practical Games

Like it or not understand that your immediate personal safety is not the responsibility of the government or law enforcement. If the goal is to be safe, it is imperative that a person trains diligently to stay safe. One must make an effort to put time and thought into the process. The hardest part of any training is getting started. I will admit, training can be tedious. In this book, I propose two kinds of training. First is preparedness training where one thinks like a predator and learns ways to counter their actions. It can and should be done anywhere. It is more of a thought process that can be practiced alone, with friends, or family. Later I propose ways to make a game out of this training so that fear is not an obstacle. The simple exercise will provide tools for everyone to use if faced with a frightening situation. The second form of training that I propose is physical. One needs to develop the muscle memory to deal with a physical confrontation. On any given day anyone can get lucky, time and chance can happen to anyone. However, training and practice provide a window of opportunity for you to be the lucky one in any confrontation.

Make Training Practical

Training and Practice is a requirement to be good at anything. Self-protection is no different. If one is not currently in a martial arts or self-defense class, I strongly suggest getting into one. Almost all of them have practical, real-world applications.

Students have problems applying techniques learned in class to the real world because they limit themselves to class rules. For example, many traditional styles like Taekwondo and karate typically do not punch to the face, so quite often practitioners of this style do not attack the head except with kicks. Brazilian Jujitsu does not attack the small joints, so they do not break fingers. When thinking of self-defense situations, think of all the weapons and tactics at one's disposal. Even if unable to practice using those techniques in class, one should explore how to apply them when training at home. Eye gouges, biting, grabbing the groin are all viable self-protection techniques. Additionally, people tend to limit their utilization of techniques to the way they train, a consequence of being unimaginative. Example, if continually training to block a punch with an outside block by moving the arm forward to intercept the strike, it is easy to lack the imagination of using the same motion in another position to block a hook or round punch. One's training should include imagining how many different variations of that technique there are. When faced with a fearful situation, there is no time to dream up new techniques. In short, you will go with what you know. Making sure that one's training contains variety ensures the ability to adapt to a fluid situation even at the height of one's fear.

A prime example of not being imaginative is while previously conducting the **"Abduction"** drill, I taught a young lady how to adjust her weight when lifted off the ground making it difficult to hold onto her. We had not trained in other ways to use her weight. The next time when executing the same drill, I did not lift her off the ground and resorted to dragging her instead. In the stress of the moment, she could only think of trying to pull away. Since I outweighed her by a significant amount, she was only able to slow my progress. She failed to imagine other methods of using her weight to free herself during the drill. This provided the perfect moment to stop and brainstorm about other tactics.

Train to Your Ability

Finally, practical training requires training effectively to maximize one's natural abilities. Every person is different. Short or tall, fat or skinny, fast or slow, every physical characteristic can be seen as both an advantage and disadvantage depending on how they are used. Be honest with yourself while training. Evaluate what is and is not practical. Do not be afraid to discard what does not work for something better. Personally, I am built like a tank, not too tall, broad, solid, and strong. I lack speed, but I make up for it in strength and intellect. I have trained to use offensive blocks and disguise my counterattacks to make them more effective.

Training to one's abilities is different from training to your strengths. Training to one's strengths is a crutch and prevents growth by focusing only on what you already do well. Training to abilities takes into account the entire scope of what one can do and builds on it. I am a strong right-handed striker. My left side is capable of the same level of power, but I am not as comfortable using left-handed techniques. Training to my abilities requires that I put in the additional time to work exclusively on my left side. Take an honest look at your abilities and add a large dose of humility. Improvement is always possible, so make plans to identify and isolate your weaknesses and strengthen them.

Practical Training Drills

I can never say this too many times, being safe requires practice and practice must be practical. I have included a copy of the drills that I use for my training and in training others. The first two drills, the **"I'm Billy Bad,"** and the **"Defensive Fence"** are the two most important. Additionally, they are also the easiest to practice and improve when in a group or alone. One can never practice these drills too often. Do not take them for granted, and assume that since they are easy and quick, they are easily mastered. Predators are always refining their craft; one should make sure to adapt and improve one's techniques.

When I perform these drills acting as the bad guy, I make sure that students understand I intend to assault them in every way possible. I am going to be loud, vulgar and violent. People who have never had someone in their face pushing them up against a wall cursing at them tend to freeze at the violence of such a drill. This is just what a predator wants to happen as it minimizes the need for physical control. It is the ideal scenario in which to train.

Now be cautious, training drills should always be safe. Make sure when practicing with friends or even an instructor there is a way to stop any drill immediately. When I teach, I make the physical portion of drills uncomfortable, but the idea is not to hurt anyone or get hurt.

During one training session in my war room, one of the young ladies was brand new to training with me, and she was not a black belt like all the others. In fact, she was several years younger than everyone else. Her biggest fear was that I would hurt her. The other girls told her, "Yes, he is going to hurt you but, if you do what he tells you, it will not hurt much, and you can get him back." Not exactly the words of comfort she was looking for.

When it came to her turn to do the **<u>Bully Beat Down</u>** drill, she was so afraid that I could practically see her heart beating through her shirt. The minute we started her she was close to panicking. Be aware of these type of scenarios. To calm her, we walked through the drill slowly so that she could see what was going to happen to her. As I recall we did about three variations of the drill before she realized that while some of the initial grabs, holds and chokes did hurt, her fear of what was going to happen was far worse than the real thing. After the first drill, and with the support of the other girls, she was willing to try all the others at full speed. Yes, she was still scared and nervous, but she kept at it. I spoke with her father a week or two later, she remembered everything and was able to demonstrate and apply what she had learned. The realism of the drills made it easy for her to visualize how to apply it.

This is the type of experience one wants to get out of these drills. When performing them with friends make sure to keep safety and learning in mind. We do not use real weapons; our sticks and bricks are foam noodles and pillows. I use rubber knives and washable markers for knife drills. The idea is to learn from mistakes, and not suffer from trying something for the first time. All of these drills have value in getting it right.

However, you can learn and grow more from mistakes. Use and enjoy your mistakes while practicing to get the drills right.

I think I have said this enough, and I say it throughout the drills, but I am going to say it again for "**that guy**," **DO NOT BE STUPID**! Safety comes first wear appropriate protection when needed. Use self-control, and stop to assess progress frequently. Everyone should understand that learning is the objective not winning. Learn what works, what does not work. Make it fun so that doing these drills should be something to look forward to.

I'm Billy Bad

Purpose	The **"I'm Billy Bad"** drill is designed to heighten a person's awareness of possible threats and see how each possible attack can be prevented, thwarted, or at least minimized. After doing this drill several times, one will notice a change in where one sits in a restaurant, how one approaches their vehicle in a parking lot, even how one pulls into their garage. This one drill will do more to improve personal safety than any other drill in this book, and the benefits are immediate.
Setup	The drill begins upon entering or settling into a new location.
Resolution	This drill ends when you have determined your reaction to each imagined form of attack.
Activity	Look at your current location and try to think like a predator. Answer the questions about an

attack, who, what, where, when, why and how. After thinking of multiple possible attacks determine how to react to each of them.

Variations This drill can be done alone but is more fun and enlightening when done as a group. Take turns thinking of different types of attacks. After a complete list is made, determine how to respond to each of them.

Warning This drill comes with a special warning, **DO NOT BE STUPID**! If sitting in a restaurant with friends talking about how someone would rob it, that looks an awful lot like a crime ring casing the place! Think before broadcasting, "If I were going to rob this place I would…"

The Defensive Fence

Purpose If violence erupts, it is going to happen within 18 inches of one's body. The **"Defensive Fence"** uses the hands to control the distance between oneself and a predator without looking aggressive. When done properly, this should allow an almost instant transition from passive defense to an aggressive counterattack.

The fence is the most crucial physical defensive technique one can learn. It is simple and effective, and as a drill, it can be practiced almost anywhere. It uses deceptive techniques to allow one to be fully prepared for violence without looking threatening. It is the best technique to use when trying to de-escalate any potentially violent situation.

Setup   Begin this drill any time or anywhere while having a standing conversation.

Resolution   The drill ends when the conversation ends.

Activity   Start with a guard stance. Do this by standing with your feet shoulder-width apart and taking one relaxed step forward. Keep the knees slightly bent, and the weight off your heels. Turn your hips until you are at an angle to the person you are talking to. The hands should be raised just below the chin the front hand directly between you and the other person. Without looking stiff or staged continue the conversation doing the following:

- Do not lower the arms past middle torso.
- Do not cross one arm behind the other.
- Use your hands while talking. Developing as many natural gestures as possible from this stance.
- Move about while keeping a distance of 18 inches or more from the person you are talking to.

Variations   Perform this drill with a training partner playing the role of a predator. Tell them about your day using this technique. At some random time during the conversation, the predator will throw a punch. Counter it and return with three or four techniques of your own.

Bully Beat Down

Purpose The idea is to simulate an assault by a bully. This drill should not last more than 30 seconds as most street fights only last 9 seconds.

Start Start with the predator threateningly grabbing the victim. This can be by the throat or lapel, and push them against a wall, or holding the victim up as if they were about to punch them.

Resolution This is a timed drill. It ends when the timer expires.

Activity Using multiple attacks strike the bully trying to disable him as fast as possible. During the counterattack, the predator should not simply let the victim attack them and do nothing. They should strike back lightly showing any weaknesses in the victim's methods. The intent is to learn and train. Minimize the amount of pain one causes to foster learning and experimentation.

Variations Alter the predator's purpose for the attack such as a thief or sexual predator. If this drill is done as a sexual predator, the predator starts much closer. Their hands can be on the victim's hips or holding them around the waist. The victim can be pinned against the wall or pulled close.

Warning THIS DRILL MUST BE CONTROLLED as the victim is trying to attack vulnerable areas of the predator. This drill can be harmful to the one acting as the predator. I recommend using protective padding and eyewear.

Home Invasion

Purpose   This is a simulated home invasion to train one's response if someone enters the home with the intent to do harm. This drill is good for school kids who are home alone and young adults who spend any time home alone. It is also good as a family activity.

Setup   The drill should have a time limit of 10 to 15 minutes, depending on one's ability to simulate a call to 911. If 911 is successfully called the drill should last no more than 10 minutes.

If there is no home phone, place one's cellphones where they would normally be during the day, it is important not to cheat on this, it needs to be accurate for assessing the time needed to reach a cell phone and call 911.

Start   Have a friend who is familiar with your home stand outside of the house and start a stopwatch on their phone. Have them walk in the back door loudly as if someone is breaking in.

Resolution   As the victim you win if you can do the following:

- Successfully leave the house without being noticed.
- Leave the house without being grabbed.
- **Simulate** a 911 call and are not found in 10 minutes **(Do NOT Actually Call 911)**.
- Are not found in 15 Minutes. One can be hidden or barricaded in a room

	• Disable or disarm the predator.
Activity	**Predator** – The predator should search the house spending time going from room to room. **Protector** – The resident upon hearing someone try to enter the home, should execute their escape or protection plan.
Variations	• Using something like a Nerf or laser tag gun, try this drill with the invader being the only one armed. Use pillows and pool noodles as makeshift weapons to fight back against an invader. • Try this drill using a Nerf or laser tag gun with both the predator and the victim armed. The victim's weapon should be stored wherever you would keep a personal firearm. The objective is to see if it can be reached in time. • If the home has an alarm, place a cellphone near the keypads with a bullhorn or siren sound file ready to play. See if one can activate the alarm before being caught. If your neighbors are the type who would come to your aid, then end the drill 5 minutes after the alarm goes off.

Abduction

Purpose   The idea of being abducted is horrifying. We often hear of kids being abducted from their yard or while walking down the street. This is a forcible act such as being dragged or kidnapped. I used a case of a grown woman taken off the street in Philadelphia.

Setup   This drill needs a distance of about 35 feet. Make a tape line at the start and end of the 35-foot stretch. Make the third line about 10-feet from the start. The victim stands on this line. This is a timed drill of about 45 seconds.

Resolution   WINNING - The victim wins under the following conditions:

- Get 10 feet on the other side of the start line.
- Disable or escape from the predator and retreat 10 feet beyond the start line
- If the timer expires, the victim wins.

If the victim is dragged or carried beyond the 25-foot line in less than 45 seconds, then they have lost.

Activity   The drill and timer start when the predator grabs the victim.

Variations   If the victim yells, deduct 10 seconds from the time. This simulates the victim attracting attention, and having someone render aid.

This is a great family drill that parents can make fun by setting up a wager to get the victim to try harder. I would have the victim wash the

	car if he or she fails, and pay for dinner and a movie if they succeed. As a parent, I want to be the loser every time.
Warning	This is a physical drill that requires padding eye protection and a cup.
	Do not hurt your partner.
Notes	For people of smaller stature trying to escape an abduction attempt, it is important to do what it takes to face the predator. If grabbed by the neck, turn toward the hand. If lifted off the ground, use the predator's arms to turn and face them.
	While physical this is a mind drill, one must first disrupt the predator's plan, then escape.

Assessing Results

With all these drills, please maintain control. Hurting someone is not the intent particularly if it is a training partner. Using these training drills provides an understanding of what is possible in similar situations while conditioning the reflexes. The training environment should be set up as a safe place to experiment and fall. A middle school student who failed the abduction drill approached me about a month later and told me she had been thinking about what she could have done differently. She had envisioned several different and more realistic responses that might work for her and was eager to try again. These drills are intended to figure out what will and will not work. With routine practice, the way one thinks will change. I use the expression every kid thinks they can fly until they meet reality. Practicing these drills is a way to test your reality and see what works, what does not, and what is just unrealistic.

Summary

There you have it, a summary of what it will take to remain safe as a youth. It requires diligence on your part, parental guidance, and a supportive community. Some of the subjects are hard to deal with, but predators count on the inexperience of youth. Knowledge and preparation are your defense.

Safety is an ongoing and personal process. Predators will always adopt new techniques, and you should constantly refine your defensive skills. If there were a magic technique that would allow one to be safe all the time, I would have shared it, but as the Kung-Fu panda learned, there is no secret ingredient!

Personal safety requires practice and consistency as does self-defense. Perform the drills, make it fun, share them with friends.

I invite you to join me on **Totalweapon.com** for workouts, more drills, and open discussions. Feel free to share your thoughts, opinions, and comments. Be blessed and be safe.

Made in the USA
Columbia, SC
21 December 2018